Postfeminist Celebrity and Motherhood

This book analyzes the intersections of celebrity, self-branding, and mommy culture. It examines how celebrity moms playing versions of themselves on reality television, social media, gossip sites, and self-branded retail outlets negotiate the complex demands of postfeminism and the current fashion for heroic, labor-intensive parenting. The cultural regime of "new momism" insists that women be experts in both affective and economic labor, producing loving families, self-brands based on emotional connections with consumers, and lucrative salable commodities. Successfully creating all three—a self-brand, a style of motherhood, and lucrative product sales—is represented as the only path to fulfilled adult womanhood and citizenship. This book interrogates the classed and racialized privilege inherent in those success stories and looks for ways that the versions of branded motherhood represented as failures might open a space for a more inclusive emergent feminism.

Jorie Lagerwey is a lecturer in television studies at University College Dublin, Ireland. Her research interests include gender, celebrity, genre, and religion on television and other digital media. Her work has appeared in *Cinema Journal, Studies in Popular Culture, Spectator*, Flowtv.org, and elsewhere.

Routledge Research in Cultural and Media Studies

For a full list of titles in this series, please visit www.routledge.com.

Postfeminist Celebrity and Motherhood
Brand Mom

Jorie Lagerwey

Routledge
Taylor & Francis Group

NEW YORK AND LONDON

First published 2017
by Routledge
711 Third Avenue, New York, NY 10017

and by Routledge
2 Park Square, Milton Park, Abingdon, Oxon OX14 4RN

Routledge is an imprint of the Taylor & Francis Group, an informa business

Library of Congress Cataloging-in-Publication Data

Names: Lagerwey, Jorie, author.
Title: Postfeminist celebrity and motherhood: brand mom /
by Jorie Lagerwey.
Description: New York: Routledge, 2016. | Series: Routledge research in cultural and media studies; 89 | Includes bibliographical references and index.
Identifiers: LCCN 2016011429
Subjects: LCSH: Motherhood. | Celebrities. | Celebrities—Family relationships. | Branding (Marketing)—Social aspects. | Mass media and families. | Feminism and mass media.
Classification: LCC HQ759 .L295 2016 | DDC 306.874/3—dc23
LC record available at https://lccn.loc.gov/2016011429

ISBN: 978-1-138-64038-2 (hbk)
ISBN: 978-1-315-63666-5 (ebk)

Typeset in Sabon
by codeMantra

Contents

Acknowledgments

I would like to thank Felisa Salvago-Keyes, Christina Kowalski, and Erica Wetter at Routledge. Thanks to Stacy Grouden and Parisa Haghshenas for their excellent administrative help. Thank you to the anonymous reviewers and Julie Wilson for providing generous, detailed, and constructive feedback on the early stages of the manuscript. Finally, thanks to my extraordinary, brilliant, kind, and generous friends for talking through ideas and reading drafts. Thank you, Suzanne Scott, Chris Hanson, Julia Himberg, Emma Radley, Taylor Nygaard, Bella Roe, Elizabeth Affuso, and Janani Subramanian, and my sister-in-law, guide and inspiration to all things mommy blogging, Hilary Lagerwey.

Introduction
Brand Mom: Celebrity, Branding, and Postfeminist Mommy Culture

In the lead up to Mother's Day 2014, an online greeting card shop created a viral video advertisement called "World's Toughest Job." In the video, the ad agency posted a job announcement for a Director of Operations, and when real applicants applied and were interviewed, the job was described as the most important job in the world and yet unpaid, 135 hours per week with no breaks, extra work on holidays, and requiring a constant "happy disposition."[1] The applicants featured in the video asked if they were allowed to eat (only after "the associate has eaten") or, indeed, if such working conditions were legal ("yeah"). Eventually, the interviewer revealed that millions of people already do this impossible job: Mothers. Rather than responding with frustration at being duped into a fake job interview, all of the applicants, men and women, looked into their computers' cameras and tearfully recounted stories of their love for their own mothers.

This type of worshipful stance toward an iconically hard-working and supposedly universal mother figure is representative of popular culture's contemporary obsession with moms. This peculiarly specific and detailed image of heroic motherhood is loving, compassionate, and devoted to her children; she may or may not work outside the home, but vitally, she works incredibly long hours in service to her family. She is completely self-sacrificing and fulfilled by the intense affective labor of this style of motherhood. This mother is intertwined with capitalist brand culture and recession; she is determinedly middle-class or upper-middle-class but never too wealthy or too poor; she is suburban rather than rural, she is in her 30s and 40s, neither too old nor too young; and she is most often white. This mother is deeply political while being represented as totally outside politics; she is repeatedly invoked to create an idealized image of an American nation. We see her in advertising campaigns like the one described above, but also in political campaigns ranging from Sarah Palin's infamous "momma grizzly" characterization during her 2008 Vice Presidential run to Michelle Obama's self-identification as "Mom-in-Chief" during her 2008–2016 tenure as First Lady of the United States.[2] More insidiously, this mother is mobilized in conservative rhetoric aimed at denying women access to contraception, health care, and reproductive choice, but she is also used by liberal politicians fighting these same policies.

This mother is a hallmark of postfeminist culture and has become an integral part of how we understand adult women in popular media from films like the mom-centered romantic comedies *I Don't Know How She Does It* (2011) or *What to Expect When You're Expecting* (2012) to self-help movements like Sheryl Sandberg's Lean In, to a slew of mothering guidebooks like *Battle Hymn of the Tiger Mom* by Amy Chua and *Bringing Up Bébé: One American Mother Discovers the Wisdom of French Parenting* by Pamela Druckerman.[3] Vitally, both Lean In and the Tiger Mom became branded transmedia commodities, thus beginning to illuminate how we understand the opportunities and requirements of women in the twenty-first century brand economy. Lean In has become a full-fledged social media movement for privileged women looking for the elusive balance of work life and family life. Amy Chua's book was similarly targeted at affluent women, but through a "model minority" lens that obscured her name throughout the book's publicity, including innumerable media appearances, speaking engagements, and a blog, in favor of the more marketable and vaguely orientalist moniker, The Tiger Mom. This image of the idealized mom manifests in mommy blogs (even those that invoke the impossibility of living up to that ideal), in celebrity mom lifestyle companies like Gwyneth Paltrow's GOOP and Jessica Alba's Honest Company, on social media sites like Pinterest and Facebook, and all over reality television.[4]

In fact, all of those manifestations are linked and built on each other. The women who attain the most wealth, fame, and longevity in the public eye do so by successfully spreading their self-brand across platforms that produce or maintain fame (like film and television), offer access or the illusion of access to a performer's "real" self (like interviews, blogs, paparazzi photos, gossip, social media, and reality television), and sell products (like lifestyle websites, promotional social media accounts, and advertising integrated into other performances). Jennifer Jones and Brenda Weber refer to this spreading of a persona, self-brand, or performance across platforms as "transmediated continuity," and, indeed, it is nearly impossible to study contemporary celebrity or television without considering all of those forms of texts.[5] For that reason, while many of the women in this book have a measure of fame (some a very small measure), thanks to reality television, my analysis of them is always situated within their transmediated continuity. Since that is not an exclusive feature of reality stardom, in addition to reality performers, *Brand Mom* devotes time, for example, to Kate Middleton, the English princess, who is famous for her royal title, her marriage, and children. The book also devotes a chapter to online lifestyle companies launched on the value of their founders' fame in fictional film and television but predicated on those stars performing versions of themselves to sell a lifestyle and an associated array of products.

This book engages with the immense privilege evident in most of these spaces and the ways in which these women's ability to create a branded self are framed as successful or not. Often, those branding successes and failures stand in for discourses of difference, including age, race or ethnicity, and religion, all of which are discussed in later chapters. The women analyzed here cultivate branded identities to navigate the contradictory demands of postfeminism, a neoliberal emphasis on individualism and entrepreneurialism, and the professional or semi-professional requirements of their media. By unpacking which women are framed as successful, which are the stars, and which are the villains of their multi-platform texts, an image emerges of what types of motherhood have the most cultural value.

This introduction will begin by setting the stage of "mommy culture," including its legal and political context in the US. Next, it explains the ways brand culture has been theorized, especially in relation to reality television and the economic and cultural value of authenticity in contemporary iterations of celebrity. From there, it will explain the ways privilege, in its gendered and classed dimensions, informs brand culture and reality TV's designations of "correct" or valuable motherhood. Finally, the chapter summaries preview specific case studies that illuminate the intersections between the mode of capitalism known as brand culture, the performed or perceived authenticity of celebrities and TV personalities, and postfeminist motherhood.

To understand why one might devote an entire book to more or less famous women performing their motherhood in popular culture, we must first understand the preoccupation with motherhood and mothering sometimes called mom or mommy culture, and its prominence in American popular culture in the early part of the twenty-first century. When I first began thinking about what would become this book, my leisure time media consumption began to be overwhelmed by mommy media (despite not being a mom myself). I watched marathon hours of reality television on the US cable channels Bravo and E!, and began to notice that the programs dominating these female-targeted basic cable brands seemed obsessed with their characters' relationship to motherhood, whether they were pregnant, struggling with fertility, mothering teenagers, or claiming to protect their children from the cameras' prying eyes by keeping them off screen. Celebrity pregnancies were big news, with tabloids devoting entire sections to "Bump Watch," closely monitoring female stars' waistlines for any telltale bulge. I also found myself losing hours to Pinterest boards dedicated to elaborate birthday cakes, homemade baby clothes, and toddler education. Friends who were new moms (and some who were not) wrote or read mommy blogs, replaced their Facebook profile photos with sonogram images of their growing fetuses and Instagrammed their babies' monthly birthdays. Mommy culture had perhaps reached its apex when the affluent, well-educated, food-, environment-, and fashion-conscious image of idealized motherhood began to be parodied on Pinterest, one of the online homes in which it thrives, in the form of Quinoa My Imaginary Well Dressed Toddler Daughter, a pinboard created by Tiffany Beveridge (Figure I.1).[6]

"Please excuse Quinoa's absence at school today. Unfortunately, she   1y
isn't feeling on brand." #MIWDTD #HOWTOQUINOA

Tiffany Beveridge

Saved to **My Imaginary Well-Dressed Toddler Daughter**

Figure I.1 Beveridge's posts feature children's fashion models and her own ironic
commentary. Hashtags #Howtoquinoa and #MIWDTD represent
the board's name so pinners can find or post their own captions of
imaginary Quinoa and her friends. Pinterest https://www.pinterest.com/
pin/27584616443363319/.

Motherhood had always been a central concern of feminist activists and
scholars, including Adrienne Rich's seminal *Of Woman Born: Motherhood
as Experience and Institution*, which arguably sparked the subfield of
motherhood studies. But, popular culture's obsession with motherhood was
booming in the 2000s and 2010s.[7] In addition, mothers in popular culture are crucial to the contemporary political landscape as women and their
reproductive choices continue to be important tools in national electoral
politics and are disproportionately affected by legislation seeking to cut
healthcare costs or limit a woman's choice to have children or not.

Contested Terrain: Pregnant Bodies as Legal Spectacle

In a hyperbolic rhetorical parallel to the international "War on Terror," US news media proliferated the phrase "War on Women" to describe conservative politicians' efforts to limit women's rights during election cycles in 2008, 2010, and 2012.[8] Republican (conservative) and Tea Party (very conservative, right wing) lawmakers campaigned aggressively throughout those years to limit women's rights on many fronts, including equal pay and parental leave policies. The most relevant battles to this chapter, however, are those that aim to enforce mandatory maternity by denying women access to contraception and criminalizing abortion. These efforts took many forms, but a vital part of the process was to codify the hypervisibility of pregnant bodies,

> At the level of policy, the insides of the pregnant woman's body are coming to have an institutionalized public status quite distinct from that of the mother, and potentially in conflict with hers; no doubt the visual publicity of these insides helps to imaginatively support the acceptance of this status.[9]

In keeping with this trend, 2011 and 2012 saw US states pass the highest number of anti-abortion provisions ever.[10] Continuing into 2014,

> lawmakers introduced 341 provisions aimed at restricting access to abortion. By the end of the year, 15 states had enacted 26 new abortion restrictions. Including these new provisions, states have adopted 231 new abortion restrictions since the 2010 midterm elections swept abortion opponents into power in state capitals across the country.[11]

In 2013, for example, State Senator Wendy Davis became a nationally recognized figure when she single-handedly blocked an anti-abortion bill in Texas with a filibuster that briefly made her a feminist heroine. Unfortunately, despite that effort, the next month the state passed a draconian bill that resulted in abortion being effectively outlawed in all but the largest cities in Texas.[12] Central to many of these laws are specific provisions about the fetus's visibility. North Dakota, for example, passed a so-called fetal heartbeat provision that banned abortions at any time after a heartbeat can be detected, around five or six weeks of pregnancy.[13] What is significant here, however, is that such a ban, in addition to outlawing termination before some women might even know they were pregnant, requires that the fetus have a heartbeat. One of the ways to detect a fetal heartbeat, particularly if an initial test fails, is to use ultrasound technology that displays the image of the fetus on a screen. The ultrasound technology makes visible the inside of a woman's anatomy, even before pregnancy is obviously visible on her body. Similarly, by 2012, Mississippi, which had only one remaining abortion provider in the entire state, had legally required women to view an ultrasound image of the fetus before scheduling a termination procedure.[14] After intense, nationally scrutinized debate about whether or not a woman could be forced to have "an invasive vaginal ultrasound" that could give a clearer picture than a standard ultrasound earlier in pregnancy, Virginia passed a law similar to Mississippi's, also in 2012.[15]

All of these restrictions operate under the assumption that a woman's reproductive body is subject to state and medical surveillance, but even more insidiously, they are grounded on assumptions about and manipulations of women's affective responses to pregnancy. The apparent assumption behind these laws is that hearing or seeing a fetus made visible will activate a woman's maternal love; that affect will and *should* overwhelm rational decision-making at that moment. Setting aside the age-old misogynistic association of women with emotion rather than reason, these laws also prioritize affect to mask the material and economic circumstances that prompt women to seek an abortion, and effectively mandate maternity.

Mandated maternity is further supported by preventing women's access to free contraception. The Affordable Care Act of 2010, known colloquially as Obamacare, originally included a provision requiring employer-funded health insurance programs to provide free-of-cost contraception to all women.[16] Obamacare suffered legal attacks and repeal attempts from many angles, but that particular provision received perhaps the most challenges. As of September 2013, the most recent count available, "100 cases have been filed challenging the rule as an infringement on religious liberty."[17] The Supreme Court came down in support of those challenges in 2014 when it granted Hobby Lobby, a craft supply store founded and owned by a Christian family, and other "closely held" corporations an exemption similar to that previously granted non-profit organizations like churches or religiously affiliated colleges and universities.[18] Taken at face value, the limits on access to contraception and abortion fit neatly into a mommy culture that celebrates motherhood as noble labor.[19] In reality, their effect is felt far more by poor women and women of color, whose reproductive bodies are already pathologized or rendered as a symptom of out-of-control bodies marked by class and race. Later chapters will unpack the ways in which mommy culture and the mode of reality celebrity under discussion are imbricated in supporting and sustaining the dominance of wealthy whiteness, but first, I examine the politics and the popular culture of contemporary mommy culture.

Mommy Culture and Popular Motherhood

At first glance, the cultural conversations that go hand in hand with all the publicity motherhood is getting at this time—about whether women can "have it all" and raise families while having lucrative high-powered professional careers—might appear several decades old. We might think of 1980s films like *Baby Boom* (1987) that address precisely these anxieties by depicting an urban-dwelling career woman who only finds true love and fulfillment when she is forced to become a mother and rebuild her financial security via a home-based craft applesauce and baby food business. But in 2012 and 2013, the conversation was still current with Sheryl Sandberg, the COO of Facebook, and Marissa Mayer, Yahoo's CEO, making headlines not only for joining the very slim ranks of women in the highest levels of corporate management, but for their writings, speeches, and policies directed at (or perceived to be directed at) female employees and young women in general. Sandberg's book *Lean In: Women, Work, and the Will to Lead* argued that women were under-represented at "c-level" (CEO, COO, and CFO positions) management because women were dropping out of the workforce, sometimes even before they became mothers, instead of "leaning in" to the workplace by negotiating for themselves both at work and at home.[20] Mayer courted controversy when one of her first moves at Yahoo was to ban flextime and working from home. Many journalists saw this move as a return "to the Stone Age," a strike against working parents, and found it particularly odd coming from a female executive, who was herself a mother.[21] One *Boston Globe* columnist wrote that Mayer was trying to "out-macho the men who run most of America's boardrooms."[22] The very idea that Mayer's management decisions seemingly could not be analyzed outside the context of her motherhood speaks to the perception of motherhood as a woman's most important role. In the same vein, Anne-Marie Slaughter, who had left her high-level position working under then-Secretary Hilary Clinton at the United States State Department, wrote a controversial article in *The Atlantic* magazine about the backlash she received for supposedly retreating from such a post.[23] In reality, Slaughter left the State Department to return to her position as a professor of politics and international affairs at Princeton University, hardly a retreat from high-powered public life to quiet domesticity, and as of 2014, she was the president and CEO of a think tank called the New America Foundation.[24] However, despite her continued paid work and high-profile public life, her article described a desire to be a more active parent as one of the reasons for leaving the State Department, spawning a rash of responses in the popular press and the blogosphere and launching an on-going "full-blown cultural discussion about the way women handle work-life integration."[25] The cultural and political valences of motherhood also receive plenty of academic attention from the likes of the interdisciplinary journal *Studies in the Maternal,* as well as a large body of media studies research about motherhood. This hotly contested question of whether women can "have it all," and what "it all" is, goes hand in hand with the elevation of motherhood to a vaunted ideal. It also reveals the privilege inherent in these conversations that assume women have the money and support to be able to make a choice between highly paid work and motherhood.

There have been many waves of mother-idolization in history, like the 1950's image of the Happy Housewife and the nineteenth century's "Cult of Domesticity."[26] Historian Rebecca Jo Plant chronicles the shift from conceiving "motherhood as an all-encompassing identity rooted in notions of self-sacrifice and infused with powerful political and social meaning" to understanding motherhood as "a deeply fulfilling but fundamentally private experience and a single (though still central) component of a more multi-faceted self" between the early twentieth century and postwar America.[27] In the same vein, in analyzing the cultural history of pregnancy, Clare Hanson notes the waxing and waning of mother worship and maintains that as "a social function, reproduction is laden with social and economic meanings, and in this context, some pregnancies are always considered more valuable, both economically and ideologically, than others."[28] In the twenty-first century so far, political rhetoric and harsh legal measures aimed at limiting women's access to reproductive health care and choice, including birth control and abortion, have had an enormously disproportionate impact on poor women and women of color.[29] This uneven impact indicates the relative value, or lack of value, of those pregnancies even in the midst of a culture celebrating the intense style of mothering inherent to the contemporary post-feminist obsession with motherhood. In the current moment, the pregnancies and forms of motherhood that are most valued are affluent white women's pregnancies and performances of motherhood, and among those, the most celebrated are those that are most brandable. Performances of motherhood that can cultivate fans or followers across media platforms and transform those fans into active consumers not just of media—although the following of content across media properties is essential in the cultivation of this kind of mom brand—but also of branded consumer products, are the most visible and celebrated forms of maternity. This tight linkage of motherhood with capitalism via reality performances and self-brands is one of the through-lines of this book.

The first critical articulation of the current cultural preoccupation with maternity may have come from Susan Douglas and Meredith Michaels a decade ago. In 2004's *The Mommy Myth: The Idealization of Motherhood and How It Has Undermined All Women*, Douglas and Michaels describe the ascendance of motherhood as the ultimate form of femininity in the wake of, and at least partially in response to, the second-wave feminist movement of the 1970s. They define what they call the "new momism" as,

> the insistence that no woman is truly complete or fulfilled unless she has kids, that women remain the best primary caretakers of children, and that to be a remotely decent mother, a woman has to devote her entire physical, psychological, emotional, and intellectual being, 24/7, to her children.[30]

The increase in discussion and promotion of attachment parenting, popularized by Dr. William Sears and Martha Sears in the 2001 book *The Attachment Parenting Book: A Commonsense Guide to Understanding and Nurturing Your Baby*, and emphasizing as much physical contact as possible between mother and child, extended breastfeeding, co-sleeping, and "no cry" responses to a child's needs, is representative of this kind of cultural promotion of motherhood.[31] Celebrities' public espousal and elaboration of their own parenting methods from attachment parents like *Big Bang Theory* (CBS, 2007–2017) star Mayim Bialik to reality TV personality Kourtney Kardashian, who tweeted a photo of Dr. Sears's book in 2012 when she was pregnant with her second child, extend the cultural currency of these parenting discussions.[32]

This insistence that motherhood is a woman's primary path to fulfillment, according to Douglas and Michaels, has become "part of our national common sense."[33] The phrasing of the May 21, 2012 *Time* magazine cover, "Are You Mom Enough?," in the parlance of a schoolyard taunt, highlights the competitive nature of the new momism and the extraordinary demands on a woman's time, physical, and emotional labor required by such intensive styles of parenting.[34] The image itself with its young, slender, pale, blonde, conventionally beautiful mom and her breastfeeding 3-year-old is meant to shock. The bold eye contact both mother and son make with the camera and therefore the viewer, presents a direct challenge to the readers. The subjects, standing against a plain white background, emphasize the (upper-) middle-classness and the whiteness of this latest glorification of maternity. In fact, part of what arrests one's attention is that this woman is already the normative ideal of motherhood, and she seems to be saying that if this is what I am doing, then so should you. The image highlights the economic and racial privilege evident in this and other representations of "good" motherhood in the 2000s and 2010s. It also shocks with a child and, moreover a boy, who is old enough to climb on a chair and easily reach his mother's bared breast, all while making knowing eye contact with the implied onlooker. The hint of sexualized taboo, combined with the normativity of the white, beautiful, middle-class mother and child, makes the image striking and controversial. *Brand Mom* examines this kind of privileged, supposedly real, mom who balances on the boundary of good taste (whiteness, wealth, and entrepreneurialism) and trash (the degraded and feminized genres of reality TV and lifestyle blogs). All of these examples foreground the prominence of mommy discourse in popular culture in the first two decades of the twenty-first century. Furthermore, they demonstrate the extraordinarily high expectations of motherhood, both in terms of culminating a woman's project of the self, as well as in the work she must devote to that ultimate achievement. But as Douglas and Michaels point out, this American cultural obsession with motherhood and mothering is, in part, a response to the feminist movements of the 1970s; just as new momism is observed in response to activist second-wave feminism, so is it imbricated in the postfeminist cultural "commonsense."

In postfeminist cultural production, in Angela McRobbie's words, feminism was successful and is, therefore, "taken into account" in contemporary representation, meaning it can be ignored, pushed aside, and discredited as an ongoing political or social project. In Gramscian terms, McRobbie argues that feminism has become part of the dominant ideology while at the same time being "repudiated, indeed almost hated."[35] In other words, the overt sexism that lends to the verisimilitude of *Mad Men*'s (AMC 2007–15) 1960's milieu would seem anachronistic in a contemporary setting, but at the same time, because that level of blatant sexism is less visible and less accepted, it is equally unnecessary and off-putting to claim to be a feminist.[36] This cultural environment accepts the gains of feminism as taken for granted, and therefore repudiates the ongoing necessity for feminist activism, and leads young female celebrities like pop singer Taylor Swift and actress Shailene Woodley to espouse equality and empowerment while insisting "I'm not a feminist."[37] This insistence that feminism is too strident, too aggressive, anti-men, and generally unnecessary grows from a more general dominance of postfeminist values.

Postfeminism is a complex, oft-defined, never entirely agreed up on set of images, cultural preoccupations, demands, and disciplines to which women must respond, all of which are entangled with culture, politics, and capitalism.[38] All three of those intertwining relationships are central to *Brand Mom*, which investigates the ways in which images of "real" moms are used to create personal brands and sell lifestyles either via advertising or consumer products. Chapter One, for example, investigates more closely these contradictory postfeminist demands on women's bodies, careers, and reproductive choices, particularly as they are enacted on "older" pregnant women's bodies.

Discourses of domesticity and retreatism, two strains of postfeminist analysis, are crucial to this discussion of motherhood, branding, and a performance of realness or authenticity on the part of greater or lesser celebrities. In the same vein as Douglas and Michaels' emphasis on domesticity and motherhood, Diane Negra describes an overwhelming discourse of "retreatism," in which professional women in popular media are shown pulling out of the paid workforce to engage in the affective labor of romance, child care, or elder care, only thereby finding full subjectivity. She argues that women "lose representability," meaning women are not visible in popular culture unless they fit one of these well-defined and delimited life-stages.[39] Emily Matchar describes a similar phenomenon citing the nostalgic lure of "old fashioned" domesticity. The surge in popularity of cooking from scratch, canning, knitting and other domestic labor, she maintains, has been refigured as crafting, micro-businesses, and leisure activities in an era anxious about employment, recession, health care, the environment, and food safety.[40] To Matchar's list of concerns, I would add anxiety about gender roles, sexuality, and marriage equality as well. While I dispute Matchar's optimistic claims that this movement toward domesticity on the part of educated, affluent, and progressive American women is "part of a shift away from corporate culture and toward a more eco-conscious, family-centric, DIY lifestyle," her book, which is a popular but extensively researched and incisive examination of this phenomenon, is a touchstone for this cultural moment.[41] In the same time frame, Kelly Oliver examines fictional filmic representations of expectant mothers and asks how pregnancy shifted from "abject," something to be hidden away from public view, to "glam," highlighting once again the hyper-visibility and adoration of motherhood in contemporary popular culture.[42] According to Angela McRobbie,

> it is not male retribution but instead the fashion and beauty system, which becomes the new authoritative regime, encouraging women to undermine their supposed threat to men based on their new wage-earning power and visibility in the public sphere through an excessive, seemingly "ironic" display of normative feminine markers such as pencil skirts, stilettos, and corset tops. Femininity is consequently naturalized on the female body, which becomes the site of identity and "self" for women in these postfeminist discourses.[43]

Pregnancy, in particular, but any ostentatious or bodily displays of maternity fall into the same category into which McRobbie puts pencil skirts and stilettos, an obvious display of femininity that undermines women's "supposed threat to men." While pregnant and maternal bodies are certainly not displayed ironically in any of the texts analyzed in *Brand Mom*, they represent the same naturalization of hyperfemininity expressed on the body and the construction of the self via those discourses of hyperfeminine display. This is in direct contrast, for example, to the way Lucy Ricardo's pregnancy appeared on *I Love Lucy* (CBS, 1951–57), when the word "pregnant" was deemed indecent for prime time audiences. Where Lucy, a prefeminist character, was forced to verbally elide her pregnancy and dress in the typically voluminous and ostensibly bump-hiding maternity fashions of her time, twenty-first century celebrity mothers wear the tight-fitting, bump-displaying fashions that show off rather than obscure the belly, rendering it not something shameful but a new growth of the body that should be displayed—a status symbol, an outgrowth of the perfect or perfectly represented female body.

Drawing on Foucault's understanding of the way power acts on bodies to define what is politically and socially productive at the time, Chris Holmlund argues that it is the cultural critic's responsibility "to define *what* kind of body this is, or what kind of bodies are needed and/or tolerated by current societies, and to describe how the apparatus of body and power functions in popular culture today" (italics in the original text).[44] *Brand Mom* intervenes in this project by illustrating some of the ways that the women who appear on these media platforms reveal the cultural value of some pregnancies and mothers over others based on demographics and their ability to understand and manipulate the economy of the self-brand. The Bravo network's careful racial and ethnic segregation of its programming; the unruliness or unfitness of older reality celebrities' maternal bodies; the classed and racialized address of celebrity lifestyle brands that evoke a star's regional home; and the TLC network's reliance on middle-classness and religious difference, to describe "normal" motherhood—all of these factors normalize the narrow confines of acceptable pregnancy and motherhood.

Motherhood, Authenticity, and Brand Culture

The cultural regime of new momism insists that women should be experts in both affective and economic labor, producing loving families, self-brands based on emotional connections with consumers, and lucrative salable commodities. Clare Hanson links the commodification of pregnancy to "a broader shift in European and American economies from material culture to consumer culture," a progression that seems to be taken a step further with the assimilation of pregnant women and mothers into brand culture.[45] There are two major components to this assimilation, the perceived necessity of a brand identity to facilitate a personal identity, and the idea that a brand identity must in some way reflect the "real" person behind it. Brand culture means that the exchange of things for money has been replaced with the exchange of "affective practices, or, as Arjun Appadurai terms it, the 'social relations of things.'"[46] Contemporary celebrity, however major or minor, also insists on an appearance of authenticity. The genres of reality TV, lifestyle brands, and the social media platforms used to promote both of them all require a performance of realness. Reality television performers are only famous for their performances of themselves, but even a major movie star like Gwyneth Paltrow, whose lifestyle site GOOP is discussed in Chapter Three, must seem to be presenting not a character, but herself when she moves from cinema screen to computer screen and lifestyle brand. Because branding relies on affective or emotional relationships between consumers and producers or companies, this idea that a brand has to be simultaneously a performance of the brand identity or brand values and of the self in order to be successful requires an intense amount of affective labor on the part of the reality TV performers and celebrity moms under discussion here.

Before continuing, it is important to define key terms in ongoing scholarly conversations about reality television and brand culture: governmentality, neoliberalism, and self-branding. Governmentality is a central concept in understanding the modes of self-performance required to create the self-brands at the heart of this book. It originates with Michel Foucault, and

> indicate[s] the degree to which governments produce citizens who are best suited to the policies of the state. This, in turn, creates a wide array of organizing and teaching practices, such as Reality TV, that participate in the governing of subjects.[47]

In other words, popular culture texts like reality television and lifestyle blogs educate viewers and consumers in dominant behavioral norms that help sustain the status quo; they teach us to fit in. In the US and Europe, neoliberalism is a common rubric by which to understand government policies that deemphasize the supportive role of the state in preference for free market and individualist solutions. Laurie Ouellette and James Hay argue that contemporary neoliberal governmentality "emphasizes self-empowerment as a condition of citizenship." They describe the neoliberal milieu, including the ways in which, as "the sense of social and financial security promised by an expanding educational system, 'jobs for life,' and guaranteed pensions comes to an end, the self becomes more important as a flexible commodity to be molded, packaged, managed, reinvented, and sold."[48] That understanding of the self as commodity leads to the notion of self-branding, which Alison Hearn argues,

> involves the self-conscious construction of a meta-narrative and meta-image of self through the use of cultural meanings and images drawn from the narrative and visual codes of the mainstream culture industries…. [I]ts goal is to produce cultural value and, potentially, material profit.[49]

Brand Mom takes this construction of a meta-image of the self, a self-brand, and examines the ways in which it is, for the affluent women discussed here, inflected by a motherhood that is itself observed to enhance cultural value and increase material profit. In a postfeminist culture that puts an enormously high value on (certain types of) motherhood, maternity is a vital component of that self to be packaged and sold. The personalities analyzed throughout this book serve as examples of the rules, limits and expectations of what it means to be successful in that drive toward full citizenship. In Chapter Two, for example, we see the ways in which the *Real Housewives of New York* and *Atlanta* (Bravo, 2008–) draw drama from watching their female stars go through the process of reinventing themselves as brands and their successes and failures in doing so. One of the pleasures of watching the *Housewives* is the tension created by some performers understanding that branding is important, but making the "wrong" choices about how to do it. New York cast member Sonja Morgan, for example, misreads the viewers' class aspirations when she attempts to launch a line of designer toaster ovens. Similarly, another New York Housewife, Ramona Singer, creates multiple products using different colors, logos, and spellings of the word True/Tru, thereby dispersing the value of her name recognition rather than consolidating it under one coherent brand identity. Furthermore, even while children are often a structuring or defining absence on the *Housewives*, it is often implied that cast members are bad or embarrassing mothers or that they flaunt insufficiently motherly bodies. All these failures stem from these women possessing inappropriate, too old, too ugly bodies, bodies that do not adhere closely enough to the idealized image of the postfeminist mommy to achieve full citizenship or subjectivity. But the women's failure lies also in their failure to internalize those rules.

That is, the humor comes, at least in part, from the idea that these women, possessed of variously unruly, undisciplined bodies, would even attempt this kind of self-branding. In this way, the *Real Housewives*, whether representing success or failure, highlights the absolute necessity for women to understand and manage their bodies and their roles as mothers, brand managers, and entrepreneurs.

The move to commodify the self in the face of neoliberal destruction of the welfare state described by Ouellette and Hay is amplified by brand culture. The distinctiveness of brand culture is its reliance, not on the simple economic principle of supply and demand but rather, on "building an affective, authentic *relationship* with a consumer."[50] Furthermore, Sarah Banet-Weiser argues, "It is through these affective relationships [with brands] that our very selves are created, expressed, and validated. Far more than an economic strategy of capitalism, brands are the cultural spaces in which individuals feel safe, secure, relevant, and authentic."[51] This idea of expressing an authentic self via identifying with or, in the case of reality performers and lifestyle gurus, by creating, a brand is central to this book's framework. While the vaguely spiritual idea of finding an "authentic self" has long been a rallying cry of self-help books, Oprah Winfrey, and her protégés, Banet-Weiser and others like Henry Jenkins, argue that in twenty-first century late capitalism, identities are formed by identifying with certain brands.[52]

While this book analyzes celebrity moms on several media platforms, reality television and the theory crafted around its relationship to the real and the ways in which it is understood as a genre are central to the understanding of motherhood analyzed here. The performativity of authenticity is perhaps most obvious on reality television, with its complex relationship to the real. Savvy reality TV viewers understand that scenes and personae seen onscreen are constructed with the help of producers and editors, yet at the same time, viewers are willing to watch with a sort of dual perspective. They have an intellectual knowledge of the genre's constructedness, recognition of the obviousness of product placement, even the occasional winking acknowledgment of that constructedness on the part of the shows themselves. But they also have a simultaneous understanding of reality performers as "real" people with whom viewers can relate as nonfictional characters sharing their lived experiences and sometimes even communicating with them directly via social media.[53] According to Brenda Weber, an "'aesthetics of authenticity' comes to mean not mimetic accuracy, but the form of mediated, distorted, and hybridized version of the 'real' that RTV [reality television] invariably offers to a larger culture."[54] I focus on the women performing this authenticity rather than those consuming those identities, but as Banet-Weiser points out, in brand culture, the relationship is reciprocal, if not equal. The connection to the real, no matter how fictitious, creates an aura of legitimacy that supports the turns toward neoliberalism, brand culture, and new momism; and the prominence of well-off white women in their 30s and 40s works to mask the privilege that is not only inherent in those identities but required for the successful ascension to full female adulthood in this cultural milieu.

Reality television in all its various forms and formats has become an essential mainstay of the US and international television industry in the same cultural moment that recentralized a heroic vision of motherhood based on affluent, predominantly white mothers. The genre recognizable in the twenty-first century as reality television has roots dating back to the beginning of the television industry with shows ranging from game shows, talk shows (all based on individual radio programs or genres before them), and *Candid Camera* (originally aired from 1948–50, the show has been revived many times with slight variations under the same title) to the proto-lifestyle show *Queen for a Day* (1956–64). In the convergence era, the proliferation of channels, screens, and the internationalization of production and distribution have made reality TV a popular, inexpensive, apparently infinitely reproducible, and therefore indispensable part of our television landscape.[55] In the introduction to their seminal collection about the genre, Susan Murray and Laurie Ouellette define reality TV

> as an unabashedly commercial genre united less by aesthetic rules or certainties than by the fusion of popular entertainment with a self-conscious claim to the discourse of the real. This coupling, [they] contend, is what has made reality TV an important generic forum for a range of institutional and cultural developments that include the merger of marketing and 'real life' entertainment, the convergence of new technologies with programs and their promotion, and an acknowledgement of the manufactured artifice that coexists with truth claims.[56]

This book takes this definition of reality television, particularly the merging of marketing discourses with self-aware artifice and simultaneous claims to the real, along with the proliferation of content across screens, and puts it in conversation with the contemporary cultural obsession with motherhood. Reality television, the nostalgia-flavored retreat to domesticity, and the star brands and lifestyle blogs analyzed here, all rely on rhetorics of realness. Mommy culture invokes the real via natural, organic, local, DIY food, clothing, and education. Its elevation of those "authentic" traits and tasks sometimes masks its nostalgic embrace of a pre-feminist past, which is itself a response to recession and growing income inequality. Reality television similarly enacts the complex relationship between audiences who understand the genre's constructedness, but simultaneously choose to understand the people onscreen as real. Reality television is also a genre of extremes, and its frequent focus on either poor and abject subjects (that is, people who disturb or contradict cultural norms or values) or the excessively wealthy, also mirrors growing economic extremes in the US and Europe. The following sections begin to explain my focus on wealthy women and the ways in which their performative excess sometimes has the potential to reveal the limitations of postfeminist brand culture.

Wealthy Moms and the Limits of Postfeminist Brand Culture

Thinking of reality television and lifestyle shopping not as feminized and degraded but as something with the same ideological functions and social value as "quality" drama can help call attention to the cultural work being done on these female-centric platforms. Throughout the book, I use Jane Feuer's term "quality reality" to refer not just to reality television but also to all the modes of self-performance I analyze.[57] The term reflects the tensions evident in these representations of privileged entrepreneurial women who lead very public lives while they attempt to embody contemporary retreatist ideals of motherhood. Quality reality, after all, is also a seeming contradiction: stylized, relatively high production values, expensive product placements, and affluent, sophisticated audiences all packaged in a "trashy" genre or a supposedly silly, frivolous pastime like shopping or lifestyle browsing. Later chapters unpack the significance of using "quality," a term so gendered and weighted with critical heft to describe debased genres like reality, celebrity tabloids and social media, and lifestyle shopping sites. But for now, continuing to question the Television Studies discourses of quality provides an ancillary reason for studying the wealthy and privileged and, hopefully, disrupting the gendered boundaries of analysis. The more central reasons for studying the privileged spaces I analyze in this book have to do with the relationship between displays of wealth and recessionary audiences, and the possibilities that contradiction produces for moving toward an emergent new phase of feminism.

Many scholars have written extensively about motherhood as represented on reality television; but most often those discussions are framed in opposition to the idealized and aspirational new momism, focusing instead on abject or bad mothers who do not have access to that ideal. In particular, much emphasis has been placed on poor and working class moms and programs like *Underage and Pregnant* (BBC Three 2009–11), *16 and Pregnant* (MTV 2009–), *Teen Mom* (MTV 2009–), and *Toddlers and Tiaras* (TLC 2009–).[58] Most existing scholarship focuses on the mothers who are too young, too poor, too fat, too fertile, and who, by counterexample, support the dominant image of an idealized white, upper-middle-class, domestic-goddess mom with restrained desires. Additionally, the focus on class might be a result of much of the work in this area having been written about British reality television, which often has a more overt focus on its performers' class positions than its American counterpart. This book adds a dimension to the existing scholarship, focusing on wealthy and celebrity women. Existing scholarship has not entirely ignored these women either.[59] So-called 'yummy mummies' and celebrity and reality celebrity moms like Kate Gosselin of *Jon & Kate Plus 8* (TLC 2007–15) notoriety; Kathy Hilton, Lynne Spears, and Dina Lohan, mothers to Paris, Britney, and Lindsay, respectively; and Mama June, the unexpectedly financially savvy matriarch of *Here Comes Honey Boo Boo* (TLC 2012–14), have all gotten scholarly attention. Whether about poor mothers or rich ones, all of the texts analyzed in this existing scholarship represent failing motherhood in one way or another. The worst punishment, as Cobb and Weber have noted, is reserved for women who are observed to have commodified their children, turning motherhood into a paid job and an opportunity for class ascension rather than the unpaid labor of love and sacrifice described in the advertisement that opened this introduction. I continue this investigation of wealthy and famous moms and the tensions between postfeminist mandates for all-encompassing sacrificial motherhood seemingly outside financial concerns, and the successful integration of the self with capitalism via the self-as-brand. As we will see in case studies throughout the book, those two demands are in constant tension, reflecting the impossibility of adhering to both.

While I explore the extremely narrow confines of body, age, race, class, and even geography in which success is defined, I focus primarily on women who are represented as "successful" postfeminist, self-branded entrepreneurs. I have chosen this focus because these women *should* represent an ideal, but they can nearly always be read simultaneously as figures of aspiration and derision. Indeed, one of the pleasures of watching these reality shows and browsing the consumer websites is to simultaneously aspire to the lifestyles on display and scoff at the excessive consumption so out of touch with recession and the ever-increasing visibility of gender, racial, and economic inequality in the nations where these shows are produced and aired. Gwyneth Paltrow's social media presence and website GOOP are perhaps the best example of this dual pleasure. The trips, clothes, and foods lovingly photographed and described on GOOP.com are gorgeous and eminently desirable (albeit wildly expensive). Flipping through the website conjures a fantasy lifestyle of ease, health, casual beauty, and conflict-free family time. At the same time, a major part of Paltrow's public persona is the contempt heaped on her self-description as a working mom and her unwillingness or inability to acknowledge her wealth and privilege. The dualities of how we understand the wealthy moms with (mostly) successful self-brands are multiple: they are performed characters but real people; they are rich and savvy but sometimes represented as "crazy;" they are idealized beauties and hideously belabored bodies; they are mothers and therefore fulfilled and complete subjects, but always treading a line between authentic motherly love and performance. The simultaneous embodiment of all of these contradictions begins to expose the failures, dissatisfactions, or ruptures in ideologically dominant versions of motherhood, postfeminism, and brand culture. As I will explore in the concluding chapter, when subjects who have achieved all of the cultural markers of success are nonetheless represented as in some way failed, or if the narrowness of success's borders are exposed too often, they can start to reveal the cracks in the ideological armor of postfeminist, motherhood-obsessed brand culture.

Because building and maintaining brands requires both cultural and economic capital, and because lifestyle brands themselves target consumers with disposable income and the middle-class taste cultures that go with that income, many of the most successful brands that have been born of reality TV come from women who already had a certain amount of wealth or cultural cachet. All of these constructions of real or authentic motherhood (discourses in which even stars like Paltrow must embed themselves when creating their consumer brand identities) are entrenched in assumptions about time, access to technology, and a level of disposable income that performs middle-class or aspirational taste cultures and ignores the reality of ever-increasing economic inequality. Undoubtedly, many of the shows, celebrities, and retail outlets discussed in this book celebrate privilege. The feuding lifestyle brands analyzed in Chapter Three, for example, sell luxury goods and an aspirational vision of wealthy motherhood even while some of them masquerade as middle- or even working-class. Wealth, whiteness, youth, beauty, and, of course, maternity are traditionally overvalued in postfeminism, and the texts studied here are no exception. If postfeminism assumes that feminism is no longer necessary because it has achieved its goals, Diane Negra and Yvonne Tasker argue that the so-called Great Recession brought with it

> a perception that equality is a luxury that can no longer be afforded. Within this formulation, the postfeminist female consumer is placed as an icon of excess as much as admiration, an emblem of the boom and a symptom of its short-term financialism.[60]

Reality performers who embody the contradiction of being aspirational figures at the same time as objects of derision in an era of intense income inequality exemplify the icons of excess Negra and Tasker describe. While the women analyzed here are figured as excessive either in wealth (like the lavish spending of the *Real Housewives* or many celebrity lifestyle companies), in body (like the labored upon bodies of reality celebrities who reveal their plastic surgery, diets, and gym time), or in family (like the mega families of TLC's religious reality shows), their representations are complex amalgams of critique and admiration, embracing the consumption and performance common to postfeminist discourse but also highlighting the strict boundaries and limitations that postfeminism places on female bodies and entrepreneurial endeavors. They are emblems of both economic boom and its desired return, as well as reminders in some ways held responsible for the massive frustrations of income inequality and a growing recognition that the aspirational, entrepreneurial, and branded self is impossible and perhaps even undesirable.

Chapter Summaries

Chapter One examines pregnant bodies in upmarket reality television and tabloid culture, and in particular, women in their thirties and early forties struggling to different extents with infertility. It elucidates the ways in which older (for childbearing) wealthy white women's pregnancies are often rendered heroic, boosting the mom-stars' presumed authenticity and often helping spread their brand across new platforms as well. Finally, by analyzing the concurrent 2012 pregnancies of English princess Kate Middleton and Armenian American reality star Kim Kardashian, I argue that the framing of celebrity pregnancies and celebrity babies reveals an image of an idealized future nation and the cultural value placed on certain pregnancies over others.

Chapter Two follows similar characters to the first chapter, but moves from pregnancy to more mature motherhood as its site of focus. This chapter examines the ways in which age and race figure into the branding of mothering identities in "quality reality" series. Specifically, it examines the brand identity of the US basic cable network Bravo and the New York and Atlanta women of its *Real Housewives* franchise as examples of its luxury motherhood brand. I argue that *The Real Housewives of Atlanta* (2008–), in particular, highlights the ruptures in Bravo's brand of postfeminist discipline and entrepreneurialism and moves the show from a vehicle for winking consumerist aspiration to an example of successful brand-selves emerging outside the strict limits of white, postfeminist, entrepreneurial success set by Bravo's other stars.

The first two chapters take reality television as their starting point but investigate the self-brands and consumer products that grow outside of those reality shows via the performers' presence online, in other television outlets, and in social media. Chapter Three takes those secondary outlets as its starting point, examining the ways in which motherhood contributes to an "authentic" identity for television and film stars to create their own personal lifestyle brands. This chapter examines the inflections of class, race, and authenticity in the promotion of these lifestyle images by analyzing the supposed feud between Gwyneth Paltrow's GOOP and Jessica Alba's Honest Company brands. It analyzes the ways in which Alba mobilizes her racialized but hybrid identity to support her own authenticity in direct challenge to Paltrow's elitist whiteness. It also explores Monica Potter's star text and online brand, Mrs. Potter, which creates a sort of authenticity exchange between her performance as a mother and activist on the TV drama *Parenthood* (NBC 2010–15) and the cultivation of her own mother/lifestyle brand online. For all of these women, their children are a marker of their down-to-earth, relatable personae that opens them to a new market. The celebrities and companies I discuss here all combine contemporary discourses of the personal or "authentic," with blogs, newsletters, or other sorts of direct address to their fan-consumers, as well as high-end or aspirational retail sales. I include these spaces because they trade in the same discourses of self-branding and postfeminist motherhood we see on the shows and in the star texts discussed in Chapters One and Two, but also because they play with the blurred boundaries of television and consumer culture that are representative of the shifting contemporary media environment.

Finally, Chapter Four leaves behind the markers of luxury and excessive wealth to focus on middle-class families. While the women discussed in the rest of the book are represented as excessive in wealth, style, or body, the women here are framed as excessive in family and faith. This chapter builds on the groundwork about network brands laid in Chapter Two, looking at a very different cable network, TLC, analyzing the religious mothers represented on TLC's *Sister Wives* and *19 Kids and Counting*, as well as their ancillary products and social media presences. TLC trades in a more educational or pedagogical mode of quality reality, using its characters' minority religious identities to support that classification. That mode of address, coupled with fringe religious identities, is mobilized to create specific images of spiritual motherhood, support TLC's brand, and create branded identities that can spark product sales for the performers outside of the shows themselves. They also plant a conservative foothold unusual in popular entertainment media. Vitally, as I discuss, it is mothers who are at the center of these narratives and who, by prodigious reproduction, are shown to be creating (or re-creating as the quaint nostalgic tone may indicate) an imagined, conservative, all white America in the face of contemporary political battles over immigration, women's rights to control their own bodies, and LGBT and African American civil rights.

Brand Mom ends with a summary of postfeminist, mommy brand culture on reality TV and lifestyle sites. It looks toward the future, however, by situating all the case studies discussed throughout the book in relation to the emerging trend of famous (especially young) women proudly expressing their feminism. Seemingly a direct response to soaring economic inequality (or at least its enormously increased visibility thanks to the recession) and tightening restrictions on women's control over their own reproductive bodies, these discourses of feminism or neo-feminism or post-postfeminism have the potential to disrupt our cultural obsession with motherhood and reject some of the limits of postfeminism. The roots of that potential, I argue, can be noticed in some of the cracks, dissatisfactions, or failures that begin to move to the fore in the quality reality programs discussed in this book.

Notes

1. Elizabeth Weiss, "Selling the Myth of the Ideal Mother," *The New Yorker*, May 8, 2014; "World's Toughest Job—#worldstoughestjob—Official Video," YouTube, April 14, 2014. Available online at www.youtube.com/watch?v=HB3xM93rXbY (accessed May 10, 2015).
2. Julie Bosman, "Provoking Palin's Inner Bear," *The New York Times*, October 19, 2008. Available online at http://thecaucus.blogs.nytimes.com/2008/10/19/provoking-palins-inner-bear/; Robin Givhan, "'Michelle: Her First Year As First Lady' Excerpt: The Mom-in-Chief Effect," *The Washington Post*, January 17, 2010. Available online at www.washingtonpost.com/wp-dyn/content/article/2010/01/14/AR2010011405324.html (accessed April 13, 2016).
3. Amy Chua, *Battle Hymn of the Tiger Mom* (New York: Penguin Books, 2011); Pamela Druckerman, *Bringing Up Bébé: One American Mother Discovers the Wisdom of French Parenting* (New York: Penguin Books, 2012); Sheryl Sandberg, *Lean In: Women, Work, and the Will to Lead* (New York: Knopf, 2013).

4. A backlash against the pervasive images of perfection has, indeed, sprung up in websites such as Pinterest Fail: Where Good Intentions Come to Die, or GOMI* Get Off My Internets, devoted to snarky critiques of mommy blogs and other fashion and lifestyle sites. Available online at http://pinterestfail.com/ and http://getoffmyinternets.net/ (accessed June 23, 2016).

5. Jennifer Lynn Jones and Brenda R. Weber, "Reality Moms, Real Monsters: Transmediated Continuity, Reality Celebrity, and the Female Grotesque," *Camera Obscura* 30.1 (2015): 11–39.

6. Tiffany Beveridge, "Quinoa My Imaginary Well-Dressed Toddler Daughter," Pinterest. Available online at www.pinterest.com/tiffanywbwg/my-imaginary-well-dressed-toddler-daughter/ (accessed February 19, 2015). See also Beveridge's presence on other social media outlets Instagram @Imaginary_Quinoa; Twitter @ImaginaryQuinoa; "My imaginary well-dressed toddler daughter," Facebook. Available online at www.facebook.com/MyImaginaryWellDressedToddlerDaughter (accessed February 19, 2015); and her book *How to Quinoa: Life Lessons from My Imaginary Well-Dressed Toddler Daughter* (Philadelphia: Running Press, 2014).

7. Adrienne Rich, *Of Woman Born: On Motherhood as Experience and Institution* (New York: W. W. Norton & Company, 1976).

8. See, for example, Al Sharpton, "GOP War on Women Going Strong," *Politics Nation*, NBCNews.com, August 20, 2013; "The War on Women," Editorial, *New York Times*, February 25, 2011.

9. Rebecca Kukla, *Mass Hysteria: Medicine, Culture, and Mothers' Bodies* (Lanham, Maryland: Rowman & Littlefield Publishers, 2005), 108.

10. The Guttmacher Institute, "Laws Affecting Reproductive Health and Rights: 2012 State Policy Review." Available online at www.guttmacher.org/laws-affecting-reproductive-health-and-rights-2012-state-policy-review (accessed July 8, 2013).

11. Elizabeth Nash, Rachel Benson Gold, Gwendolyn Rathbun, and Yana Vierboom, "Laws Affecting Reproductive Health and Rights: 2014 State Policy Review," *Guttmacher Institute* (undated). Available online at www.guttmacher.org/statecenter/updates/2014/statetrends42014.html (accessed February 12, 2015).

12. The bill "bans abortions after 20 weeks of pregnancy, requires abortion clinics to meet the same standards as hospital-style surgical centers and mandates that a doctor have admitting privileges at a hospital within 30 miles of the facility where he or she performs abortions." Manny Fernandez, "Abortion Restrictions Become Law in Texas, But Opponents Will Press Fight," *New York Times* July 18, 2013; see also Manny Fernandez, "In Texas, a Senator's Stand Catches the Spotlight," *New York Times*, June 26, 2013; Anna M. Tinsley, "Restrictive Law Could Cause Most Texas Abortion Clinics to Close," *Star-Telegram*, July 6, 2013.

13. Five or six weeks is the earliest ban in the country, and the law was overturned by a federal court; the state is appealing to have the law reinstated, a decision that was still pending in 2015. Erik Eckholm, "Bill in North Dakota Bans Abortion after Heartbeat is Found," *New York Times* March 15, 2013. Available online at www.nytimes.com/2013/03/16/us/north-dakota-approves-bill-to-ban-abortions-after-heartbeat-is-found.html. See also Tara Culp-Ressler, "North Dakota, Home to Nation's Strictest Abortion Law, Approves Yet Another Ban for Good Measure," ThinkProgress.org, April 17, 2013 (accessed June 23, 2016).

14. "Inside Mississippi's Last Abortion Clinic as It Faces Closure," BBC News Magazine January 22, 2013. Available online at www.bbc.co.uk/news/world-us-canada-21150116 (accessed July 8, 2013).

15. Erik Eckholm and Kim Severson, "Virginia Senate Passes Ultrasound Bill as Other States Take Notice," *New York Times,* February 28, 2012.
16. United States Department of Health and Human Services, "Affordable care act and the Title X Program." Available online at www.hhs.gov/opa/affordable-care-act/index.html (accessed April 13, 2016).
17. "Challenges to the Federal Contraceptive Coverage Rule," ACLU.org, January 6, 2015. Available online at www.aclu.org/reproductive-freedom/challenges-federal-contraceptive-coverage-rule (accessed April 13, 2016).
18. A closely held corporation means a private business without publicly held shares. Adam Liptak, "Supreme Court Rejects Contraception Mandate for Some Corporations: Justices Rule in Favor of Hobby Lobby," *New York Times,* June 30, 2014. Available online at www.nytimes.com/2014/07/01/us/hobby-lobby-case-supreme-court-contraception.html (accessed April 13, 2016); Burwell v. Hobby Lobby Stores, Inc. No. 13–354 (2014). Accessed via Legal Information Institute, Cornel University Law School. Available online at www.law.cornell.edu/supremecourt/text/13-354#writing-13-354_OPINION_3 (accessed April 13, 2016).
19. In 2015, the Obama administration found a way around this ruling by passing on contraceptive costs to insurers even if employers would not pay on religious grounds. Laura Bassett, "White House Finds Way Around Hobby Lobby Birth Control Decision," *Huffington Post,* July 10, 2015. Available online at www.huffingtonpost.com/2015/07/10/white-house-birth-control_n_7771004.html (accessed April 13, 2016).
20. Sheryl Sandberg, *Lean In: Women, Work, and the Will to Lead* (New York: Knopf, 2013).
21. Jenna Goudreau, "Back to the Stone Age? New Yahoo CEO Marissa Mayer Bans Working from Home," *Forbes,* February 25, 2013.
22. Joan Vennochi, "Yahoo's Broken Glass Ceiling," *The Boston Globe,* February 28, 2013.
23. Anne-Marie Slaughter, "Why Women Still Can't Have It All," *The Atlantic,* June 13, 2012.
24. New America Foundation. Available online at www.newamerica.org/experts/anne-marie-slaughter/ (accessed April 13, 2016).
25. See, for example, Jodi Kantor, "Elite Women Put a New Spin on an Old Debate," *New York Times,* June 21, 2012; Sandra McElwaine, "The Accidental Feminist Icon," *The Daily Beast,* November 15, 2013. Available online at www.thedailybeast.com/witw/articles/2013/11/15/anne-marie-slaughter-on-her-new-america-job-and-becoming-a-feminist-icon.html (accessed April 13, 2016); Kelsey Wallace, "Anne-Marie Slaughter in *The Atlantic*: 'Women Still Can't Have It All': Can Anyone?" *Bitch Magazine,* June 21, 2012. Available online at http://bitchmagazine.org/post/anne-marie-slaughter-in-the-atlantic-feminist-magazine-women-work-life-balance-children-career (accessed April 13, 2016); Julie Zeilinger, "Why Anne-Marie Slaughter Thinks We Need a 'Men's Movement,'" *The Huffington Post,* July 23, 2013. Available online at www.huffingtonpost.com/2013/07/23/anne-marie-slaughter-mens-movement_n_3639846.html (accessed April 13, 2016).
26. Emily Matchar, "From Angels in the House to Crunchy Domestic Goddesses: the History of 'Women's Work,' *Homeward bound: Why Women Are Embracing the New Domesticity* (New York: Simon & Schuster, 2013), Kindle Edition, 29–46.
27. Rebecca Jo Plant, *Mom: The Transformation of Motherhood in Modern America* (Chicago: University of Chicago Press, 2010), 2–3.

28. Clare Hanson, *A Cultural History of Pregnancy: Pregnancy, Medicine and Culture, 1750–2000* (New York: Palgrave-MacMillan, 2004), 37.
29. Susan A. Cohen, "Abortion and Women of Color: The Big Picture," *Guttmacher Policy Review*, 11.3 (Summer 2008). Available online at www.guttmacher.org (accessed April 13, 2016); Tara Culp-Pressler, "Unintended Pregnancies Are Increasingly Concentrated among Poor Women Who Lack Birth Control Access," *Think Progress*, September 9, 2013. Available online at http://thinkprogress.org/health/2013/09/09/2593011/unintended-pregnancies-poor-women/ (accessed April 13, 2016); Eyal Press, "The Abortion Rate Is Declining—for Some Women," *The New Yorker*, February 11, 2014.
30. Susan Douglas and Meredith Michaels, "Introduction," *The Mommy Myth: The Idealization of Motherhood and How It Has Undermined All Women* (New York: Free Press, 2004), Kindle Edition.
31. William and Martha Sears, *The Attachment Parenting Book: A Commonsense Guide to Understanding and Nurturing Your Baby* (New York: Hachette Book Company, 2001). See also askdrsears.com and Matchar's summary of the parenting philosophy in *New Domesticity*, 23–4.
32. See, for example, Bialik's blog on the Jewish parenting site kveller.com. Available online at www.kveller.com/mayim-bialik/ (accessed May 28, 2014); Kourtney Kardashian, @kourtneykardash, "Excited to read http://instagr.am/p/NkL7OGE1g4/," July 26, 2012, 6:12pm, Tweet. See also Alicia Silverstone, *The Kind Mama: A Simple Guide to Supercharged Fertility, a Radiant Pregnancy, a Sweeter Birth, and a Healthier, More Beautiful Beginning* (Emmaus, PA: Rodale, 2014).
33. Douglas and Michaels, "Introduction."
34. Kate Pickert, "The Man Who Remade Motherhood," *Time Magazine*, May 21, 2012.
35. Angela McRobbie, "Post-feminism and Popular Culture," *Media Studies: A Reader*, 3rd ed., eds. Sue Thornham, Caroline Bassett, and Paul Marris (New York: NYU Press, 2009), 351.
36. For two revealing analyses of postfeminist media products nostalgically Imagining a prefeminist past, see Jennifer Clark, "Postfeminist Masculinity and the Complex Politics of Time: Contemporary Quality Television Imagines a Prefeminist World," *New Review of Film and Television Studies* 12.4 (August 2014): 445–62; Lynn Spigel, "Postfeminist Nostalgia for a Prefeminist Future," *Screen* 55.4 (Winter 2014): 270–8.
37. Eliana Dockterman, "Shailene Woodley on Why She's Not a Feminist," *Time Magazine*, May 5, 2014; Ramin Setoodeh, "Taylor Swift Dishes on Her New Album 'Red,' Dating, Heartbreak, and 'Grey's Anatomy,'" *The Daily Beast*, October 22, 2012.
38. Yvonne Tasker and Diane Negra, "Introduction: Feminist Politics and Postfeminist Culture," in *Interrogating Postfeminism: Gender and the Politics of Popular Culture*, eds. Yvonne Tasker and Diane Negra (Durham, NC: Duke University Press, 2007), 1–26. See also Rosalind Gill, "Postfeminist Media Culture: Elements of a Sensibility, *European Journal of Cultural Studies*, 10.2 (2007): 147–66.
39. Diane Negra, "Postfeminism, Family Values, and the Social Fantasy of the Hometown," *What a Girl Wants?: Fantasizing the Reclamation of the Self in Postfeminism* (London & New York: Routledge, 2009), 15–46; 47–85.
40. Emily Matchar, *Homeward Bound: Why Women Are Embracing the New Domesticity* (New York: Simon & Schuster, 2013), Kindle Edition.

41. Matchar, "The Pull of Domesticity in an Era of Anxiety," *Homeward Bound*.
42. Kelly Oliver, *Knock Me Up, Knock Me Down: Images of Pregnancy in Hollywood films* (New York: Columbia University Press, 2012), 2.
43. Jessalynn Marie Keller eloquently summarizes McRobbie in her essay, "Fiercely Real?: Tyra Banks and the Making of New Media Celebrity," *Feminist Media Studies* (2012): 3, Online First Edition (accessed September 20, 2013).
44. Chris Holmlund, *Impossible Bodies: Femininity and Masculinity at the Movies* (New York: Routledge, 2002), 5.
45. Hanson, 174.
46. Sarah Banet-Weiser, *Authentic™: The Politics of Ambivalence in a Brand Culture* (New York: New York University Press, 2012), 71. See also Arjun Appadurai, *The Social Life of Things: Commoditites in Cultural Perspective* (Cambridge: Cambridge University Press, 1986).
47. Brenda Weber, "Trash Talk: The Gender Politics of Reality Television," *Reality Gendervisions: Sexuality and Gender on Transatlantic Reality TV*, ed. Weber (Durham, NC: Duke University Press, 2014), 26–7.
48. Laurie Ouellette and James Hay, *Better Living Through Reality Television: Television and Post-Welfare Citizenship* (Malden, MA: Blackwell Publishing, 2008), 7.
49. Allison Hearn, "'Meat, Mask, Burden': Probing the Contours of the Branded 'Self,'" *Journal of Consumer Culture* 8.2 (2008): 198.
50. Banet-Weiser, 8.
51. Ibid., 9.
52. Henry Jenkins, *Convergence Culture: Where Old and New Media Collide* (New York: New York University Press, 2006), 20; see also Henry Jenkins, "Affective Economics 101," *Flow TV* 1.01 (September 20, 2004).
53. MTV's *The Hills* (2006–10) finale, for example, spoke to the consistent rumors that its conflicts and storylines were manufactured by staging a dramatic farewell between two of its romantic protagonists and then pulling the camera back to reveal that the entire scene was shot on a studio backlot and that the Hollywood sign visible in the background was, in fact, a movable photographic backdrop. "All Good Things" Episode 6.12, Originally aired July 13, 2010.
54. Brenda Weber, "Trash Talk," 20.
55. For an analysis of reality TV's importance to the international TV industry and its cultural significance around the globe, see the excellent collection *Global TV Formats*. Tasha Oren and Sharon Shahaf, eds., *Global Television Formats: Understanding Television Across Borders* (New York and London: Routledge, 2012).
56. Susan Murray and Laurie Ouellette, "Introduction," *Reality TV: Remaking Television Culture*, 2nd ed., eds. Susan Murray and Laurie Ouellette (New York, New York University Press, 2009), 3.
57. Jane Feuer, "'Quality' Reality and the Bravo Media Reality Series," *Camera Obscura* 30.1 (2015): 185–95.
58. See, for example, Imogen Tyler, "'Chav Mum, Chav Scum': Class Disgust in Contemporary Britain," *Feminist Media Studies* 8.2 (June 2008): 17–34; Tyler, 'Pramfaced Girls: The Class Politics of "Maternal TV,"' *Reality Television and Class*, eds. Helen Wood and Beverly Skeggs (Basingstoke, UK: Palgrave Macmillan, 2011), 210–24; Tyler, "Pregnant Beauty: Maternal Femininities under Neoliberalism," *New Femininities: Postfeminism, Neoliberalism and Identity*, eds. Rosalind Gill and Christina Scharff (Basingstoke, UK: Palgrave,

2011); Letizia Guglielmo, *MTV and Teen Pregnancy: Critical Essays on* 16 and *Pregnant and* Teen Mom (Toronto: Scarecrow Press, 2013); Laurie Ouellette, "'It's Not TV, It's Birth Control': Reality TV and the 'Problem' of Teen Pregnancy," *Reality Gendervision: Sexuality and Gender on Transatlantic Reality Television*, ed. Brenda R. Weber.

59. See, for example, Jo Littler, "The Rise of the 'Yummy Mummy': Popular Conservatism and the Neoliberal Maternal in Contemporary British Culture," *Communication, Culture & Critique* 6 (2013): 227–43; Shelley Cobb, "Mother of the Year: Kathy Hilton, Lynne Spears, Dina Lohan and Bad Celebrity Motherhood," *Genders Online Journal* 48 (2008); Brenda Weber, "From All-American Mom to Super Bitch from Hell: Kate Gosselin and the Classed and Gendered Politics of Reality Celebrity," *Reality Television and Class*, eds. Helen Wood and Beverley Skeggs (London: Palgrave Macmillan, 2011); Kirsten Pike, "Freaky Five-Year-Olds and Mental Mommies: Narratives of Gender, Race, and Class in TLC's *Toddlers and Tiaras*," *Reality Gendervision: Sexuality and Gender on Transatlantic Reality TV*, ed. B. R. Weber.

60. Diane Negra and Yvonne Tasker, "Introduction: Gender and Recessionary Culture," *Gendering the Recession: Media and Culture in an Age of Austerity*, eds. Diane Negra and Yvonne Tasker (Durham, NC: Duke University Press, 2014), 4.

1 Branding Baby
Incorporating Conception and Pregnancy into the Self-Brand

In May 2015, *Entertainment Weekly* (*EW*) published its "2015 Baby Power List."[1] Mimicking *Forbes Magazine*'s annual World's Most Powerful People list or *EW*'s own annual ranking of celebrities with the most Hollywood clout, the Baby Power List ranked the top 10 celebri-babies of the year, with Prince George, son of the Duke and Duchess of Cambridge, playing the royalty card to edge out victory over the merely wildly famous North West, daughter of musician Kanye West and reality personality Kim Kardashian, who nabbed the second spot. This list may have been tongue in cheek, but contemporary popular culture is in the throes of mommy mania, and the most important accessory to the successful maternal subject is a gorgeous on-brand baby. Movie stars, TV stars major and minor, and, of course, mommy bloggers and every woman who wants to fit the dominant norms of complete and fulfilled middle- or upper-class womanhood in the 2000s, all have them. Rachel Zoe, for example, a celebrity stylist and star of the reality show that documented her businesses and family foibles, *The Rachel Zoe Project* (Bravo 2008–13), demonstrated her carefully branded bohemian style and professional skill in selecting clothes for her own pregnant frame throughout her show's fourth season. Then, as her infant son Skylar grew into a toddler on season five, Zoe dressed him in elaborate, expensive, designer clothing, always impeccably accessorized. In essence, baby Skylar became a walking advertisement for his mom's styling business, advertising luxury brand names in the adorable child package so amenable to mommy culture. This chapter analyzes reality celebrity pregnancies, specifically challenging pregnancies, often ones that follow infertility melodramas played out onscreen and in ancillary texts like gossip blogs and magazines. These infertility stories and pregnancies, as well as the resulting children, whether highly celebrated or notorious, are culturally and economically over-valued. By analyzing the shifts in women's performance of self and cultivation of brand during and after difficult pregnancies, I elucidate the ways in which reality and tabloid celebrity pregnancies reveal that wealthy white women's pregnancies are often rendered heroic, boosting the mom-stars' presumed authenticity and often their brand as well. The valorization of this version of pregnancy and motherhood is only heightened in contrast to poor and minority women's pregnancies circulating in the same media. Pregnancies on

Teen Mom (MTV 2009–), or *I Didn't Know I Was Pregnant* (TLC 2008–), for example, which feature young, often poor or working class women, are devalued or pathologized in contrast to the celebrated children of the wealthy and famous.

Those images of pregnancy indicate the "correct" ways to be a fully realized postfeminist subject in a brand culture where feminism might be reemergent but is not yet realized. I will also examine the ways in which the pregnancies interact with the reality performers' and other stars' performances of authenticity and cultivation of self-brands defined as successful by their ability to spread across platforms. For the reality performers and tabloid celebrities in this chapter, motherhood is represented as not just the path to a complete self but also, in some sense, itself a new platform over which to spread a self-brand. The lengthy, often melodramatic narratives devoted to the emotional and physical work necessary to conceive and carry a difficult pregnancy to term imbue these mothers with an added level of heroism that can lend a brand gravitas and longevity, and paint a rather clear picture of which pregnancies are the most valuable and which the least.

By closely examining the hypervisibility of pregnant women in "quality reality" TV and accompanying tabloid gossip, this chapter explores why some pregnancies are represented as successful and natural, and others as unruly or alienated. In an era of increasingly harsh limitations on American women's access to reproductive choice and health care, difficulty conceiving actually renders a woman a more gallant mother for enduring physical and emotional pain to indicate just how essential motherhood is to fulfilled womanhood, and how valuable certain modes of motherhood are in contemporary popular culture. All of these factors are dependent on and are rooted in the hypervisibility of pregnant bodies, which is a relatively recent development. The chapter begins by rooting the twenty-first century visibility of pregnant bodies in a brief historical and cultural context. After examining reality performers and their challenging pregnancies, the final section extends the idea of a self-brand to the idea of a national brand, comparing the simultaneous 2012–13 pregnancies of reality mogul Kim Kardashian and English princess Kate Middleton. The divergent representations of these two pregnancies, as well as the infants North West and Prince George, hint at nationalized images of idealized maternal citizens and the idealized future citizens they parent.

If You've Got It, Flaunt It: Pregnancy Becomes Public Spectacle

In 1952, US broadcast television saw its first "real" pregnancy when star Lucille Ball's actual pregnancy was written into the storyline of her fictional alter ego Lucy Ricardo on *I Love Lucy* (CBS 1951–57). The word "pregnant," evidently deemed too crass for broadcast, was replaced in all of the scripts with the more vague and apparently more palatable, "expecting." The second season episode that announced Lucy's pregnancy was titled "Lucy Is *Enceinte*," and Lauren Berlant maintains that the French evokes something both exotic and sexualized, a marked contrast from the linguistic censorship and voluminous, body-hiding pregnancy fashions of the day. Berlant further notes that the show's sponsor, tobacco company Philip Morris, had to be convinced to allow the star to incorporate her pregnancy on the show. Ball's husband and producing partner Desi "Arnaz had to argue ... that the pregnancy in the private domestic space of the Ricardo Family might actually increase consumer identification with the family, the show."[2] From the first, then, onscreen pregnancy was linked to branding and Arnaz recognized the affective impact pregnancy could have on viewers' bond with the show and the affiliated sponsor's brand. When that brand shifts from a tobacco company to a performer's self-brand, the connection between performer, (mediated) pregnancy, and viewer arguably only becomes more powerful. In the intervening sixty years since Arnaz's battle with Philip Morris and the exotic use of French to describe Lucy's condition, pregnant bellies have become hypervisible, and with that visibility have come distinct changes in their cultural status.

After Ball/Ricardo's 1952 maternity sitcom, scholars seem to agree that the next benchmark in the history of media pregnancies is Demi Moore's August 1991 *Vanity Fair* magazine cover.[3] In the image, Moore, nude save for an enormous diamond ring and matching earrings, cradles her distended belly with one hand, covering her breasts with the other, and stares proudly into the camera. Standing against a black background and lit with coppery light, the actress seems to smolder off the page looking directly at the consumer. Jo Littler marks this cover photo as the beginning of the now widespread "yummy mummy" (or MILF, in the American) trope sexualizing pregnant and newly maternal women.[4] Certainly, it serves as shorthand support for Kelly Oliver's argument that pregnancy has gone from "abject" to "glam" in the space of just a few short decades. The baring of Moore's pregnant belly is highly sexualized, but her nudity also makes her fecundity as visible as it could possibly be, making the pregnant belly literally a public commodity to sell magazines. This situation is entirely in keeping with Douglas and Michaels' "new momism," a cultural moment that mandates maternity and a mother's utter devotion "physical, psychological, emotional, and intellectual," to her child, but it also demonstrates the extraordinary breadth of the shift in cultural understandings of pregnancy from Lucy to Demi.[5]

Clare Hanson argues that pregnant bodies are "doubly mutable," subject to physical change as well as shifting cultural interpretations, which she links to scientific, medical and national discourses that all work to make the womb more public and more visible.[6] Tracing the cultural history of pregnancy from the mid-eighteenth century to 2000, she argues that as "a social function, reproduction is laden with social and economic meanings, and in this context, some pregnancies are always considered more valuable, both economically and ideologically, than others."[7] Before the widespread use of birth control, women were expected to bear about eight children in their lifetimes, which meant that the future of the family did not rely on any individual pregnancy or resulting child. So medical texts in the eighteenth century emphasized the health of the mother over that of the fetus, expecting that every family would lose at least one child in miscarriage or infant illness. Contraceptive knowledge became widespread at the beginning of the twentieth century, at a time when social commentators were also worried about declining overall birth rates. This combination, along with medical advances in maternity and neonatal care, led to a shift in emphasis to the health of the fetus over the health of the mother.[8]

Changes in the visibility and public meanings of pregnant bodies are also related to evolving media genres like reality TV and online gossip, as well as screen technologies themselves. Philosopher Rebecca Kukla argues that the publicizing of formerly personal ethical, religious, medical, financial, and simply practical decisions surrounding every stage of conception and pregnancy started to become public at the end of the eighteenth century and at the beginning of the nineteenth century because it was around that time when medical science determined the exact anatomy and precise functioning of women's reproductive system. The idea of the "uterus as public theater," she writes, was advanced with the invention of X-ray and ultrasound imaging that literally made visible the inside of a woman's body. Reproduction was thus moved from the realm of the private and personal and made subject to the clinical, medical, and masculine public gaze.[9] Notably, the X-ray and ultrasound technologies that facilitated this shift are early documentary screen technologies. They bear an indexical relationship to the real, which reality television certainly draws on in its claims (however negotiated) to authenticity in its representation of supposedly real people. Indeed, reality performers' pregnancies are rendered more credible by the onscreen display of the very ultrasound technology that Kukla describes. It is commonplace in reality TV pregnancy storylines, just as in their fictional counterparts, to confirm pregnancy with an onscreen, tearful but joyous ultrasound procedure. In fact, thwarting that expectation by putting a woman trying to conceive in a medical environment and denying the expected image/resolution helps drive home the representation of infertile women's bodies as unnatural, too old, unhealthy or otherwise tragic. Pregnant bodies and the fetuses they carry thus become, via this hypervisibility, essentially public entities to interpret politically, legally, and culturally. Furthermore, they blur the physical boundaries of a woman's body, making the belly available even for physical touch and interpretation in public.

Once a woman's body becomes pregnant, regardless of the woman's personal feelings, the public at large seems to consider the belly public domain. Memoirist Rachel Cusk actually recounts the loss of her privacy as one of the most affecting results of her pregnancy.[10] In the same vein, women's magazines, mommy and parenting magazines and websites, and innumerable pregnancy blogs have addressed the issue of "Belly Etiquette: To Touch or Not to Touch?" (Verdict: Never touch without permission, even close friends can find this invasive).[11] This violation of privacy and transformation of bodies into public goods when they become visibly pregnant is one dimension of the ways in which fertile bodies are overburdened with public meaning.

The prioritization of maternal health versus fetal health and of individual privacy versus public visibility of fertile bodies has waxed and waned; however, in the 2000s, conservative domestic politics in the US have pushed hard against access to safe and legal abortion, clearly favoring fetal health over that of mothers. The strident anti-abortion rhetoric coming from conservative politicians who are overwhelmingly white and male and whose policies indisputably support wealthy constituents at the expense of others is difficult to separate from changing birth patterns. After the 2010 census, the US Census Bureau announced in 2012 that "non-Hispanic whites now account for a minority of births in the US for the first time."[12] The links between contemporary demographic and political realities and popular culture representations are complex, multi-valent, and far from direct. Nonetheless, the contradictory impulses that emphasize the difficult pregnancies of wealthy white women on upmarket reality television, while pillorying ethnically marked or poor women's pregnancies in tabloids or on lower-budget, less "quality" versions of reality shows, all seem to be responding or reacting to this same mix of cultural and political phenomena.[13]

Women's reproductive bodies are consistently the terrain on which ideological battles are represented and fought. In writing about *Homeland* (Showtime, 2011–), Alex Bevan argues that women's sexualized and reproductive bodies are the territory on which unrepresentable contemporary warfare, so often a matter of remote controlled weapons or digital tracking, is rendered visible.[14] The same holds true for domestic political battles. Women's fertile bodies become the way to render visible the invisible or politically unspeakable notions not just of which pregnancies should be supported or valued but also of racial and class-based hierarchies of what demographics of motherhood are framed as heroic, and which are unruly, undisciplined, or undesirable. Within the individualist, neoliberal, and brand-saturated culture described in the introduction, the most valued public pregnancies are those that fit into, or better yet, expand, a pre-existing self-brand.

The persistence and pervasiveness of mommy culture can sometimes mask the ways different pregnancies and motherhoods have different cultural meanings. The remainder of this chapter analyzes reality celebrities who have difficulty conceiving and, therefore, sink enormous resources of cash, time, and emotion into that process. It also examines famous women for whom pregnancy itself is uncomfortable, a health risk, or makes them the target of tabloid vitriol. By examining the representations of women for whom pregnancy is thus de-naturalized, the naturalization and even mandating of maternity are thrown into relief. In the process of challenging the "natural" process of conception and birth, these women's performance of fertility melodramas reveals the interdependence among women's bodies, brands, and maternity in this particular cultural moment.

Fertility Melodramas

Melodrama and self-branding both rely on affect to be effective. Peter Brooks's classic definition of melodrama cites "the indulgence of strong emotionalism; moral polarization and schematization; extreme states of being, situations, action; overt villainy, persecution of the good, and final reward of virtue; [and] inflated and extravagant expression" as essential elements of the mode.[15] Linda Williams has called melodrama a body genre because of the embodied reactions—tears—those elements create in viewers.[16] In a similar reliance on affect, branding depends on the consumer's love and trust in a person or company such that she is willing to follow the brand across multiple platforms and fork over hard-earned cash to buy the products it sells or endorses. Melodrama then, a mode that exploits viewers' emotions and elevates the goodness of its virtuous characters, is a perfect vehicle for brand expansion. For reality celebrities, the affect created by a melodramatic narrative adheres to the performer's self-brand because, after all, the character who is finally rewarded for her suffering and virtue is a real person, performing a version of herself. Two reality performers, Rachel Zoe and Giuliana Rancic, serve as examples of the ways in which difficult pregnancies boost a brand at the same time that they indicate which pregnancies are the most economically and culturally valuable at a time of economic and social crisis.

Ordinarily, female bodies are subject to the rigorous discipline and rejection of pleasure required to maintain the slender and contained body ideal described by Susan Bordo in her seminal work on the meanings of women's bodies, *Unbearable Weight*.[17] Reality television's governmentality typically enforces this body discipline.[18] Additionally, it frequently monitors and fetishizes fertility with programs like *Jon & Kate Plus 8* (TLC 2007–11), *19 Kids and Counting* (TLC 2008–), and even the TV version of the online tabloid *TMZ* (Syndicated 2007–). These shows and their tabloid and entertainment news cousins extend the idea of the pregnant body as a public good subject to not just legal and medical surveillance but also the surveillance of popular culture. On shows that transform pregnancy into entertainment, conceiving and bearing children become not just reproductive labor but labor that produces a lucrative commodity: the entrepreneurial mother.[19] By commodifying their fertility or their fertility struggles, the performers are often rewarded with opportunities to spread their brand across platforms in much the same way as they have spread their genetic code to the next generation. When female reality performers act out their inability to conceive onscreen, the evident emotional, financial, and physical investment in becoming pregnant renders the resultant motherhood even more worthy of celebration and praise than a typical birth within new momism. That excess value builds that mom's brand, and as we will see when we discuss Kim Kardashian and Kate Middleton at the end of the chapter, those most valorized motherhoods create an image not just of an idealized upper class mom but of a nation's idealized next generation.

Writing about Paris Hilton's, Lindsay Lohan's, and Britney Spears's moms, Shelley Cobb describes the ways in which bad celebrity mothers are villainized for being seen to profit from their children's fame. She argues that "a woman's identity as a mother and as a working person are perceived to be mutually exclusive, as opposed to the masculine ideal in which having a job means being a good father."[20] When the focus is transferred from motherhood to conception, however, in certain strict confines, incorporating motherhood into a self-brand can be framed as heroic, and in entertainment news presenter Giuliana Rancic's case, literally lifesaving. In the 2010s, at the same time as the political sphere was rife with discussions of women's right to abortion and contraception and the inevitable accompanying rhetoric about the sanctity of life, there was a cycle of female-centered reality programs that featured stories of women who were not yet mothers but desperately desired to be. In some instances, this took the form of young women like Kim Kardashian (before her 2014 marriage to Kanye West) bemoaning her lack of a lasting romantic relationship and expressing a fervent desire to have children as soon as possible. There was also a set of programs starring white women in their mid-to-late 30s and early 40s, characterized as older for childbearing. These women range from TLC's religious mothers like Meri Brown from *Sister Wives* (TLC 2008–) or Nonie Williams of *My Five Wives* (TLC 2013–), to wealthy entertainment professionals like the aforementioned Giuliana Rancic or celebrity stylist Rachel Zoe. In the infertility melodramas acted out on their respective reality shows, *Giuliana & Bill* (E! 2009–), and *The Rachel Zoe Project* (Bravo 2008–2013), and their ancillary gossip and popular press texts, that relationship is revealed to be more complex when put in conversation with the multiple impossible demands postfeminist mommy culture puts on women to be idealized slender bodies, self-branded entrepreneurs, and simultaneously practice the intense style of motherhood idealized by the new momism.

Both Giuliana Rancic and Rachel Zoe have personal brand identities that pre-date their reality shows; however, for each of them, the difficult road toward conceiving a child redeems their "unnatural" status as working women and non-mothers, and in the process, the emotional language of melodrama aligns them with feminized affect rather than the masculinized world of profitable work. Within the confines of mommy culture, the emotional language of melodrama actually enhances their credibility as postfeminist entrepreneurs and helps enable the spread of their brands beyond television and their initial businesses onto other platforms. Both Zoe and Rancic had at least some pre-existing fame as a sought-after celebrity stylist and an entertainment news presenter, respectively. Both women also illustrate the ways in which the impossibilities of living under the postfeminist regimes of female identity are written on women's bodies. They are extremely slender and are subject to constant speculation about their weight and health in the tabloid press. In her analysis of female bodies and their literal and cultural weight, Susan Bordo discusses the value placed on restraining the very appetites that the unruly woman exposes. A hunger for food, she maintains, has long stood in for a woman's sexual appetite. Controlling a woman's food consumption operates as an internalized Foucauldian discipline, training "female bodies in the knowledge of their limits and possibilities."[21] Alongside this insistence on discipline and limits is its counterpart, the representation of fatness as lack of control and downward social mobility. On *Teen Mom*, for example, Amber, the only overweight cast member, plays the role of "archetypal Bad Mother."[22] Similarly, on TLC's "redneck reality" show *Here Comes Honey Boo Boo* (TLC 2012–14), Kirsten Pike argues that

> pregnant and fat female bodies are repeatedly held up as objects of scorn and ridicule…. Thus, while *Honey Boo Boo* carves out a much-needed cultural space for dialogue about women's health, it also problematically casts teen pregnancy and obesity as the gross and laughable side effects of 'white trash' women and girls.[23]

It would seem that public celebrations of maternity might offer a 40-week-long escape from the rigorous discipline and rejection of pleasure ordinarily required for women to maintain the slender and contained body ideal. After all, a distended pregnant belly is not only license to "eat for two" but also puts a woman's sexual and reproductive body clearly on display. Rancic, in particular, however, highlights the double bind in which entrepreneurial postfeminist women like Zoe and her often find themselves. For both women, the emotions that come with fertility treatments, whether spoken or not, create excesses that spill beyond the text to be interpreted and speculated on by other media, but which also demonstrate the impossibility of existing within each separate postfeminist demand: slender-contained body, self-branded entrepreneur, and mother.

Rachel Zoe is a short, vanishingly slender woman with a tousled mop of long blond hair and signature over-sized sunglasses. She grew up in New Jersey and began her fashion career in New York, but she speaks with the vocal fry, rising inflection, and exaggerated vowels that sound more surfer or valley girl than New Yorker, and mark her accent as thoroughly LA. Jane Feuer notes her "encoded Jewish Princess demeanor," but I would argue that Zoe very carefully cultivates a persona that is equal parts fashion-obsessed airhead, relying heavily on the Zoeisms Feuer notes "('die,' 'kills it,' 'literally,' 'ohmygod,' 'shut it down,' 'bananas,')" and whipsmart businesswoman.[24] Zoe's deadpan delivery and frequent use of exaggerated blinks to indicate someone has expressed an opinion so bizarre she cannot comprehend it, or exasperated eyerolls (often at her husband's expense) in the confessional segments denote an irony and self-awareness that clearly signal her reality show persona as performance. Not even Zoe's layers of ironic armor, however, can protect her from the intense pressure to become a mother.

Throughout season three of her show (2010), Zoe visited fertility specialists and talked about her struggle to get pregnant. Her doctor, without discussing any specifics on the air, referred obliquely several times to Zoe's "health" being a factor in preventing her pregnancy. Zoe never explained what that meant during the show, but there was rampant speculation in tabloids, gossip sites, and comment threads that she was simply too skinny to conceive or carry a child.[25] Without ever acknowledging whether her weight was an issue, Zoe was eventually able to conceive with the aid of undisclosed medical intervention, and subsequent seasons of the show feature her son Skylar. Pregnancy not only forced Zoe to gain weight and conform to disciplinary body norms in that way, but the baby then became an extension of Zoe's fashion-based brand.

In addition to enacting the double bind faced by women trying to conform to slender body ideals and the demand for motherhood at the same time, Zoe is essentially bullied into becoming a mother. As seen on early seasons of *The Rachel Zoe Project*, Zoe is not interested in having a child. Her husband, in contrast, wants children badly and exerts continuous pressure on her, resulting in a show that often frames Zoe as somehow disordered because she does not embrace the desire for children. In a season three episode, Zoe is tasked with cooking a Passover Seder for her visiting family. Throughout the episode, Zoe's incompetence in the kitchen doubles for the unnaturalness of her not wanting children. Zoe eventually fobs off the cooking on helpers, saying that she will make the salad, which she proceeds to arrange with impeccable artistic precision in a giant terracotta bowl as she describes the way food is a visual experience, all about color, just like fashion. On a professionalized, mixed gender cooking show like *Top Chef* (Bravo 2006–), such comments would indicate a chef's mastery of presentation; in this context, they are framed as ditziness or frivolity, used to highlight Zoe's prioritization of work over domestic life and her equation of everything in her life with fashion. Toward the end of the episode, she has a conversation with one of her assistants, Joey, in which she reveals that she is terrified of having a child. Evoking the emotional trauma and sacrificial motherhood common to women in melodrama, she wonders if she is emotionally strong enough to deal with pregnancy's potential complications and physically strong enough to carry a child to term. This moment disrupts Zoe's usually glib, self-aware performance, a deflection she acknowledges when she tells Joey, "I just make jokes when I talk about having a baby."[26] Zoe also gets pressure from her sister and parents, and in a to-camera confessional interview in the following episode, her husband Rodger Berman says, "I probably won't stay in this relationship," if she continues to prioritize work and not agree to have a child.[27] Zoe's representation enacts the time panic and the emphasis on work life balance that Diane Negra argues is typical of postfeminist romantic comedies.[28] Even more so, the pressure to have a baby is a pressure to retreat from work life and to incorporate motherhood into her brand in conformity with recession era new momism. Additionally, the conjunction of Zoe's baby anxieties with medicalized concerns about her weight, her own questioning of her physical strength, alongside her career and the show's emphasis on fashion, renders the conflict thoroughly embodied. At the center of all of these contradictions and conflicts is Zoe's own unnatural, frail, too skinny body.

This discourse only retreats when her son Skylar is born and Zoe's fashion obsession and conflicts between work life and home life are reconciled through him. Zoe is still caught in a double bind. While she is rewarded with preserving her marriage, making her family happy, and having some scrutiny taken off her own body, the reliance of her family on her work is still elided. Instead, her family chastises her for working too much or using her son as a fashion mannequin and, therefore, expanding her brand through him—a criticism similar to that faced by the bad celebrity mothers Cobb described. Yet Zoe embraces this new narrative. Nearly half of the *Rachel Zoe Project*'s final episode is devoted to Zoe talking about how having a son transformed her life and made her a more complete person. But her brand is still a primary concern. In that final episode, husband Rodger buys Skylar some "normal" clothes—rock band t-shirts, jeans, sweat pants, and a trucker hat—so that he can look like a "tough" "normal boy."[29] In the to-camera interview intercut with the scene, Zoe says, "I don't think Rodger understands the importance, nor does he care, and he just wants Skylar in, like, a Grateful Dead t-shirt and a pair of jeans." In signature Zoe style, the line delivery could be ironic, but the fact that the show's production team organized a shopping trip for Rodger so that this scene could happen indicates the obvious importance of Skylar's wardrobe to the expansion of Zoe's brand from stylist to the stars to entrepreneurial mother with hair salons, her own fashion label, and a line of accessories, in addition to her show and accompanying blogs, appearances, and promotional materials.

Zoe went on to have a second child, demonstrating the completeness of her transformation from unnatural female entrepreneur to entrepreneurial mother. As of 2015, Zoe had mastered the art of incorporating baby into brand, hiding both the work of motherhood and the work of running multiple businesses and spreading a brand across platforms behind a beautifully crafted social media presence with the constant use of hashtags like #skylarmorrison #kaiusjagger (her children's names) #mommymoments and #familytime celebrating her motherhood and family. From a reality show portraying her as an (albeit comically) unnatural, career-focused, childless woman in her 40s to an Instagram feed full of photos tagged #familyiseverything, Zoe has fully incorporated her maternity into her self-brand and used it to grow followings on these platforms where work photos and ostensibly private family photos are intermixed at random intervals with equal weight, growing her self-brand and further diminishing any distinction between performances of motherhood and displays of her work. Zoe's emergence into and embrace of

mommy culture reinforces the notion that no matter how financially successful, no postfeminist woman can be complete without children. At the same
time, it merges motherhood, self-branding, and entrepreneurialism in a fairly
seamless example of making brand baby work for brand mom.

Reality star Giuliana Rancic offers an interesting counterpoint to Zoe's
example. Her brand, rooted more in goofy likability and apparent authenticity than Zoe's sun-glasses covered, Botox-filled, pre-baby cynicism, does
not incorporate her child into her brand as comprehensively as Zoe either.
Rancic's fertility drama, while like Zoe's is inextricable from postfeminist
discourses of the body, troubles those discourses by allowing Rancic to
directly address the impossibilities of inhabiting both a mothering body and
the publicly traded body of an entertainment professional. Rancic began as
a presenter on the entertainment news program *E! News* (E! 1991–) in 2006
with subsequent long-term roles on the network as a red carpet interviewer
and panelist on the snarky celebrity commentary show *Fashion Police*
(E! 2002–). On *Giuliana & Bill* (E! 2009–), Rancic stars with her husband
Bill, himself a reality TV alumnus and winner of 2004's first US season of
The Apprentice (NBC 2004–). Giuliana (I use first names for the remainder
of this section to avoid confusion between husband and wife) is the daughter
of Italian immigrants, and Bill, who grew up in Chicago, embodies a down-
to-earth Midwestern practicality. Their wealth is on constant display as they
commute back and forth between homes in Los Angeles and Chicago, buy
and remodel a new home in an affluent city center Chicago neighborhood,
and invest in new business ventures. Nonetheless, their ethnic and regional
identities, emphasized by Bill's Chicago sports fandom and apparel or Giuliana speaking Italian with her parents, lend them a whiff of middle-class
approachability that sets them apart from the wealthy women of Bravo's
Real Housewives franchise, for example, who are simultaneously figures of
aspiration and scorn. So, while their wealth protects them from the classed
abjection heaped on fat bodies like *Here Comes Honey Boo Boo*'s Shannon
family, they mobilize their regional and ethnic identities to create an image
of a loving, supportive partnership made up of two self-branded entrepreneurs (Bill relies on motivational speaking and appearances for at least a
part of his income) who are wealthy but operating within certain boundaries to prevent slippage into representations of excess. That is, Giuliana is
skinny and pretty, Bill is physically fit, they talk constantly about maintaining their budget, even if that budget is far beyond the reach of the average
viewer, and their family has not grown beyond one child.

That last detail is important because while motherhood is mandated by
mother-obsessed contemporary popular culture, fertility itself can be read
as excessive when mothers are seen as having too many children to support without government assistance or without exploiting their children for
profit.[30] We can see this in action with the backlashes against Kate Gosselin
of *Jon & Kate Plus 8*, subsequently *Kate Plus 8* when she divorced her
husband (TLC 2007–11), and Nadya Suleman, whom the press dubbed
Octomom in 2009 when she gave birth to octuplets, in addition to the

six children she already had. *Teen Mom* (MTV 2009–) and *Here Comes Honey Boo Boo* (TLC 2012–15) represent specifically classed, though still predominantly white, young women as struggling and unfit mothers, and Suleman's pregnancy and motherhood are pathologized because of their perceived excess, her poverty and reliance on government support programs, and because of her much-discussed alleged use of plastic surgery to make herself look like canonized celebrity mother Angelina Jolie.[31] Kelly Oliver points out that Kate Gosselin was similarly punished in the tabloid press because of her pre-fame class status, the excessiveness associated with the number of children she had—first twins and then sextuplets—and her oft-captured onscreen temper.[32]

In *Giuliana & Bill*'s fourth and fifth seasons, which aired in 2011 and 2012, the Rancics try to get pregnant. When they are not initially successful, they see a fertility specialist. Giuliana's inability to conceive is treated with medical scrutiny, including unsuccessful intrauterine insemination (IUI), followed by hormone shots to prepare for in vitro fertilization (IVF), and frequent doctor's visits. During one of these clinic visits, there is an offscreen conversation between the doctor and Bill, in which the doctor apparently tells Bill that Giuliana needs to gain weight to conceive and carry a pregnancy to term. In the following several episodes, the "prescription to gain five pounds," as Bill calls it, carries the weight of medical diagnosis but is rendered strangely personal by the doctor's refusal to say it on camera and thus the transferral of medical authority from doctor to husband. Furthermore, according to what is visible in the text of *Giuliana and Bill*, all of this takes place out of Giuliana's earshot and verifiability, making her subject to a ruling she has not witnessed. Over the next several episodes, Bill attempts to force Giuliana to eat and reiterates that she must gain weight to conceive.

Thus, even before conception, Giuliana is represented as an unnatural skinny body that cannot support a pregnancy. In a move unusual in reality television, or indeed in any aspect of postfeminist culture, Giuliana acknowledges her extreme slenderness and repeatedly explains the importance of being very thin to her career as an entertainment news host. Revealing the interconnectivity between fashion, entertainment industries, and beauty norms, and implying their centrality to understandings of postfeminist success, Giuliana tells her husband that she is required to fit into the sample-sized dresses provided for her appearances, especially on the red carpet, and that she must maintain a certain look to keep her job as an entertainment news host. Bill repeatedly responds that career cannot be considered more important than conception (despite his own demanding work and travel schedule), continuing to insist she gain weight.

What is elided in these exchanges is the couple's reliance, at least in part, on Giuliana's paid labor on E! as well as on this very reality show for the money not only to live their upper class lifestyle with homes in Los Angeles and Chicago, but also to pay for expensive fertility treatments. Furthermore, it is Giuliana's brand identity and connections to the E! network that garnered the couple this reality TV contract. The ability to do that remunerated labor is directly linked to Giuliana's body and ability to stay very skinny. In this instance, the maintenance of her ready-for-television self-brand seems to prevent her achieving postfeminist success via motherhood, revealing the impossibilities of adhering to postfeminism's contradictory demands.

In-between reality show seasons, Giuliana's inability to conceive is further pathologized and medicalized by the revelation that she has breast cancer. Her fertility specialist required her to have a mammogram before undergoing IVF, and it was this mammogram that discovered the cancer. In this reality storyline then, infertility and childlessness are tied directly to disease, and a desire to pursue motherhood regardless of the financial and emotional costs or threats to one's career, literally saves Giuliana's life. Nonetheless, in the wake of a double mastectomy and additional cancer treatments, Giuliana was unable to continue with fertility treatments and the Rancics ended up using what they referred to as a gestational carrier (often called a surrogate). The emotional trauma of this fertility melodrama played out in the text of *Giuliana & Bill*, as well as in promotional interviews and Giuliana's breast cancer awareness speaking engagements during the show's hiatus before their son Duke was born in 2012.

Rancic's case is particularly interesting because while her work as an entertainment news presenter, red carpet interviewer, and fashion commentator puts her adjacent to a world of glamorous celebrity and requires her to dress in expensive fashions similar to those worn by her Hollywood interview subjects, she functions as a stand in for a mass audience. Similarly, her self-branded fashion line, G by Giuliana is sold not in high-end boutiques but on the Home Shopping Network. Prices, ranging from less than $20 for clearance sale items to well over $100, are also available on Flex Pay, an installment payment plan that encourages women to buy clothing not strictly within their budgets and frames fashion as a tool for upward mobility. Again, her immigrant roots and links to Midwestern wholesomeness and practicality (via her husband) allow her to function as a sort of liaison between aspirational consumers and the luxury lifestyle her self-brand is simultaneously adjacent to and outside of. Son Duke has become part of this self-brand as the axis around which Bill and Giuliana now argue about the correct ways to spend money. Bill plays his role as sensible Midwesterner battling Giuliana's silly extravagance when it comes to baby clothes, toys, and birthday parties. For baby Duke's second birthday, for example, Giuliana proposed scaling back and hosting his cousins at a trampoline park rather than the cowboy-themed extravaganza that marked his first anniversary. Tabloid *Us Weekly* reported,

> When it comes to this year's party, Giuliana is prepared to tighten the purse strings—to the delight of her business-savvy husband, 43. 'The most important thing is getting friends together and doing something fun. It doesn't have to cost a lot of money. I'm sounding like my husband right now: His favorite word is "budget,"' she told *Us* with a laugh.[33]

Rancic and Zoe provide examples of valorized, wealthy, white motherhood, and demonstrate the untenable contradictions of postfeminism played out on women's bodies. On the one hand, it could be seen as a welcome relief for women viewers to see mandatory motherhood, the slender body ideal, and the demand for self-supporting entrepreneurialism battle each other to a stalemate in these reality shows, star texts, and self-brands. On the other hand, the ultimate resolution for each is salvation through motherhood. This image is supported by the implied (albeit negotiated) authenticity of reality performance as well as the aspirational elements of these shows. So, in contrast to the mostly unrepresented but always implied craven, immoral women who stopped or ended life with contraception and abortion, the enormous expense, physical pain, and emotional turmoil of the women struggling with infertility on the public stage of reality television are amplified. Furthermore, the tropes of melodrama like tight close-ups that emphasize crying or pained faces, swelling musical cues that evoke tension, worry, or sadness, and a heightened sense of the consequences and import of banal actions and decisions, function to give these stories extra emotional impact. Because branding, and especially self-branding, relies entirely on affective connections between consumers and performers, we can see how the heightened emotionalism of melodrama pays off in cold, hard, economic terms as well. Fertility melodramas strengthen the bond of sympathy and affection or even identification between consumer and brand and might drive viewers to cross platforms and become consumers. At the very least, these melodramatic stories travel exceedingly easily across platforms. Zoe, because she was a minor celebrity and wished to keep her fertility private, did not make talk show appearances or grant interviews to news outlets and so was fodder for gossip. Rancic took a different strategy and turned her fertility drama and subsequent health scare into an opportunity to promote discussions of breast cancer treatment and to destigmatize surrogacy. This action earned the couple enormous goodwill, as reflected in their reality show staying on the air despite network ownership changes, the death of their original network, and even allegations of racism against Giuliana when she made an off-color joke on one of her other jobs, *Fashion Police*. (Giuliana survived that scandal with a quick and seemingly heartfelt apology.) Rancic and Zoe's difficult pregnancies both illustrate the ways in which motherhood is framed as essential to fulfilled adult womanhood. Indeed, within mommy culture, the expense and emotional drama that lead to children frames them as extra heroic and their children as especially economically and culturally valuable. Both women's fertility struggles are directly, textually linked to the requirements of their jobs, indicating the impossibility of conforming to all the conflicting demands of entrepreneurialism and motherhood inherent to the postfeminist, recession era pressures on women to withdraw from the workforce and retreat to domesticity. Incorporating babies into the self-brand, however, can reconcile some of those tensions by rehabilitating an aging brand or a brand too high end for recession era audiences (Zoe) or by emphasizing a brand's "normalcy" and approachable likeability (Rancic).

Class, Race, and the Future of the Nation

These reality stars' self-aware performances of authenticity mark their texts as aspirational and even inspirational stories of overcoming odds to achieve the ultimate goal of motherhood. In the process, they enshrine affluent, white motherhood as so important that one should, indeed, invest intense emotional labor and money into achieving it despite the obstacles, a status bolstered by the contrast to unruly or excessive mothers marked by class or a deviant ethnicity like Kate Gosselin or Nadya Suleman. In this section, I examine the ways in which similar difficult pregnancies create excesses of meaning that spill beyond the text into understandings of nation and citizenship, examining the ways in which public pregnancy plays out when attached to bodies with specific racial, ethnic, or national identities through the tabloid discourses surrounding the simultaneous 2012–13 pregnancies of Armenian American reality celebrity Kim Kardashian and English princess Kate Middleton.

While tabloid culture is a departure from the "quality reality" programs discussed thus far, it is relevant here because gossip relies on the same discourses of disciplining surveillance and the dual address to consumers who read tabloids simultaneously for a glimpse of "the real," and with an understanding that "the real" being presented is often manipulated by both the producers of gossip and the stars themselves. Tabloid gossip is also a reality TV paratext, as well as a symbiotic parasite; gossip and reality TV are financially dependent on each other via their content. Tabloids add to the body of knowledge about a performer or a show, reinforcing or challenging representations or brand identities formed in reality shows or other media. But gossip also keeps that performer in the public eye, helping to create and maintain their celebrity, without which, of course, the reality show would lose ratings and the performer would lose fans. Tabloids and reality TV are, in essence, different components of the same machine. We have already seen this at work, briefly, in the cases of Rachel Zoe and Giuliana Rancic and the ways in which tabloids and online gossip speculated about their weight and health issues before and during their first pregnancies. Additionally, both this style of reality TV and tabloids rely on viewers' or readers' dual understanding of the texts as both artificial but linked to the real, often through the very bodies of the personalities on display. In keeping with mommy culture, Sylvia Hewlett's *Baby Hunger* argues that professional women, coded as middle- and upper-class white women, are putting off pregnancy and motherhood too long and deeply regretting that choice. Kelly Oliver characterizes that argument as a eugenic message urging that "white women should have babies before it is too late," and describing the very few pregnant black women in Hollywood films as surrounded by circumstances of violence, abjection, and horror as in 2009's *Precious*, a pattern we see repeated in the dearth of black women's pregnancies on reality television and the violence or abjection that often surrounds lower-class white pregnancies on programs like *Teen Mom* or *Here Comes Honey Boo Boo*.[34] The valorized affluent white women's pregnancies common on high-end reality television, especially put in contrast to mothers othered by poverty or race, continue this essentially racist message elevating white pregnancies above others. This situation becomes even clearer, perhaps, when we examine two pregnancies with national and even global audiences.

Coincidentally, Kim Kardashian and Kate Middleton, also known as Catherine, Duchess of Cambridge, or Princess Kate were pregnant with their first children at precisely the same time in 2012–13. Indeed, US gossip magazine *Us Weekly* even speculated on its cover that they were "Due the Same Day!"[35] Notably, just above the headline, a pink-colored box on that edition's cover read "Kate vs. Kim" and side-by-side photos showed the slim princess, grinning at the camera but otherwise in ¾ profile, wearing a demure pastel yellow dress complete with be-ribboned fascinator. Meanwhile, Kardashian was photographed head on, with a straight face, and in a form-fitting, long-sleeved white dress. The headline's subtitle reads, "It's a Royals vs. Reality Showdown: The nurseries, the baby clothes, their bump style & baby weight battles. Inside the exciting last month." This image and headline set the two women in contrast to each other, but most importantly, the "vs." that appears twice on the cover, and the use of the word "battles" to describe each woman's weight gain clearly sets them in opposition and competition with each other and with their bodies. This manufactured competition forces highlights of the things that distinguish each woman from the other, and the result is a tabloid discourse of weight and fashion burdened by unspoken assumptions of ethnicity, nation, and class.

Both Kardashian and Middleton are wealthy, image-savvy women, and like Zoe and Rancic, maintain carefully constructed self-brands rooted in fashion, style, and attitude. Like Zoe, Kardashian plays herself as ditzy, work-obsessed, and somewhat aloof from everyday life. Her labor-intensive hair and makeup are professionally done (typically off camera, unless the scene is a photoshoot) every day. She is frequently photographed in designer fashions, and her first business that was not based on building, maintaining, and exploiting her fame is DASH, a clothing boutique she owns with her sisters. Like Rancic, Middleton portrays herself as approachable and cheerful. Her royalty prohibits Rancic's goofiness, but Middleton is almost always seen smiling and waving at a crowd or playing with or caring for children. She is often photographed playing sports as part of her charitable activities, and she typically wears casual hair and minimal makeup. In fact, Middleton famously did her own makeup for her 2011 wedding, a gesture at middle-class normalcy rendered somewhat meaningless by her custom couture Alexander McQueen gown, Westminster Abbey setting, and royal groom. Where Kardashian, at least on *Keeping Up with the Kardashians* (E! 2007–), is constantly working, Middleton is the anti-professional, having given up her career aspirations for the public appearances and charity work required of her royal role, and the postfeminist dream title of Her Royal

Highness.[36] Her "commoner" status and fashions that are often affordable (or at least occasionally attainable luxuries) for middle-class royal watchers lends to her careful cultivation of the image of an Everywoman. Of course, behind that image lies immense privilege. Her "averageness," and with it her whiteness, represented so often by her broad, gleaming smile and the flowing brunette hair indicated by her occasional Internet moniker Princess Shinylocks, is enshrined in centuries of English aristocratic privilege.[37] Furthermore, her child, heir to the throne, is painted as a collective, public child not just of the people for whom he will one day be a figurehead leader, but of royal watchers around the world. The baby is rarely the singular Will and Kate's baby, but almost always the more collective "The Royal Baby." One commenter in *The Guardian* newspaper, in reference to a family portrait released shortly after the baby's birth, remarked on the artificiality of the young royal family's cultivated averageness, calling it an "obvious fiction" that nevertheless reassured the public in uncertain economic and political times. "They have nothing to worry about," he writes, "So maybe if we identify with them, we have nothing to worry about either."[38]

Like Zoe and Rancic, and indeed her own late mother-in-law Princess Diana, Middleton was attacked for being potentially too skinny to conceive or carry a child to term.[39] While there was no public record of her having any trouble conceiving, her pregnancy was medicalized by her first trimester hospitalization for hyperemesis gravidarum, an extreme version of morning sickness.[40] Nonetheless, alongside the pathologization of her slender frame (which tabloids had already attributed to the extraordinary stresses of being a newly minted princess, including "kidnap threats, grueling etiquette training, worry over her sudden weight loss, and demands for a royal baby"), Kate was celebrated, with headlines like *The Independent*'s "Born to Rule" and *Daily Mirror*'s "Our Little Prince," as the mother of a nation's future.[41]

While both Kardashian and Middleton attempt to cultivate images of normalcy that are "obvious fictions," the sharp contrast between the treatment of Kate's and Kim's simultaneous pregnancies was not just about the obvious aristocratic and national status one had and the other lacked— Kim, in fact has built her post-sex tape career on being an "authentic" personality rather than the privileged daughter of well-known parents and a famous step-parent—but also fraught with representations of Kardashian's pregnant body as excessive, unruly, and inappropriately on display that are rooted in her exoticized ethnic identity.

Kim Kardashian, and by extension the entire extended Kardashian/ Jenner clan (mom Kris Jenner, now former step-parent Caitlyn Jenner, sisters Khloe and Khourtney, brother Rob, half sisters Kylie and Kendall, and step-brother Brody Jenner all appear on *Keeping Up with the Kardashians*) were awarded their first TV show and their first family-wide fame not because of their late father's notoriety as OJ Simpson's defense attorney nor because of step-parent Jenner's former Olympic glory, but because Kim appeared in a widely circulated sex-tape with minor pop star Ray J. Thus, her fame grew from and continues to be, to a large extent, located in her body rather than in any skill or specific personality trait. In their discussion of the Kardashian media empire as representative of the gendered dynamics of post-recession class discourses, Maria Pramaggiore and Diane Negra situate Kim's curvaceous body, and specifically her large butt, as part of the "long tradition of racial and ethnic fetishization that spans Sarah Baartman, known as the Hottentot Venus, and Jennifer Lopez."[42] Writing about "Jennifer Lopez's body-oriented publicity" and in particular photographers' and the entertainment press's fixation on her large butt in the early years of her career, Mary Beltrán argues that nonwhite stars are particularly salient in their function as definers of power and identity "given that social and racial hierarchies are both reflected in and reinforced by a nation's system of stardom."[43] Beltrán writes about Lopez's crossover Latina stardom, and the Kardashian's ethnically marked whiteness operates in a somewhat different register, but the intense focus on Kardashian's embodiment, coded as excessive in size and sexuality (at least in part because of the origin of the family's media fame in Kim's sex tape), works in the same way to negotiate the boundaries of white identity and the social and racial hierarchies Beltrán discusses. Within the *Keeping Up With the Kardashians* media universe, while the frequent mentions of the Kardashian family's Armenian heritage serve to exoticize the sisters' beauty, Pramaggiore and Negra point out that "At the same time, the women overtly signal aspirations toward a convincing whiteness through, for example, multiple series mentions of the importance of hair removal."[44] The harsh disciplining to which Kim Kardashian's pregnant body is subject in the tabloids is centered around her body not as exotic, but as excessive, with headlines like "I'll Eat As Much as I Want," "65lb Weight Gain!," "Don't Call Me Fat!," and "I'll Never Be Sexy Again."[45] Kardashian's excessive body was frequently contrasted to Middleton's too-slender body with headlines such as *You* magazine's "Kate the Waif vs Kim the Whale."[46]

It is these tensions, between exoticism and the banality of Kardashian's domestic reality sitcom that spends endless hours rehashing familiar, mundane family squabbles; between marked ethnicity and invisible whiteness; that open Kim Kardashian's pregnant body to a harsh tabloid discipline opposite to that which Zoe, Rancic, and the Duchess of Cambridge are subject. Her otherness is even further inflected by her partner Kanye West's blackness and the tabloids' reinscription of racialized stereotypes about West's dandyism and deadbeat black dads in their insistence that he had first counseled her poor fashion choices and then abandoned her while pregnant for being too fat.[47] The triumphant post-baby reclamation of her curvaceous but slender body, combined with the ultimate fulfillment of her postfeminist self by becoming a mother, go some way to reconcile the multiple modes of Kardashian's unruliness. Nonetheless, only her daughter North West can fully reconcile those tensions by becoming an integral part of her mom's brand.

In contrast, when Middleton's baby, Prince George, and eventually her second child, Princess Charlotte, appear in tabloid snaps and supposedly casual family photos published in the national press, their blond, chubby-cheeked whiteness paints a false image of middle-class normalcy for the young royals. It also enshrines a vision of the future of the UK as sunlight-drenched whiteness, masking the sinister celebration of privilege in adorable baby pictures. The royal children are thus mobilized not just to help brand the Duke and Duchess of Cambridge as "regular" people and Everyman rulers but also to firm up a certain vision of the nation in the face of economic crisis that foregrounds class division and racist anti-immigration sentiments. Post-2008 recession austerity policies that limit access to health care and education and cut back on other social services continue to pave the way for political alternatives like the left leaning Scottish Nationalist Party (SNP) and challenges to the continued coherence of the UK, such as the failed 2014 Scottish independence referendum. At the same time, as has happened in many European countries, they have heightened the popularity of right wing parties like the United Kingdom Independence Party (UKIP) that has expanded its anti-European Union base with harsh anti-immigration rhetoric. In this context, Middleton and her children (again echoing Princess Diana and her children in the Thatcherite 1980s) function as an ideological bulwark against a nation in crisis.

But if Prince George and his sister Charlotte are the cherubic vision of ancestral white authority, Kim Kardashian's multi-racial daughter North West is celebrated as a vision of harmonious post-racial America. Baby North is not subject to the vitriol aimed at her mother's ethnically marked excessive body. Instead, her designer-dressed, lovingly Instagrammed toddler body is celebrated as part of a future America that is not burdened by its institutionalized racism and the anti-black violence so prevalent in the 2010s. Anthony McIntyre has written about the ways in which actress Zoey Deschanel's cuteness is used to neutralize her political activism and, in particular, her feminism.[48] These babies—as well as other celebrity babies, notably the Jolie-Pitt family and the slew of single white Hollywood actresses who have recently adopted black sons—celebrity figures in their own right, function similarly.[49] Their globalized fame overburdens their images with meaning, but their downright adorableness masks the need for contemporary social change by envisaging a future in which royalty is just like the middle-class or multi-racial children erase white supremacy by their very existence.

In some ways, Kardashian, and even more so her daughter North West, are bridge figures. Jane Naomi Iwamura develops the idea of a bridge figure in relation to orientalist representations of Eastern religions in US culture. Bridge figures signify tensions within a dominant culture, laying claims on both dominant and marginalized identities. "Ultimately, ... [they] represent future salvation of the dominant culture—they embody a new hope of saving the West from capitalist greed, brute force, totalitarian rule, and spiritless technology."[50] Rather than saving America from capitalist greed and spiritless technology, baby North West symbolically battles the brute force of American racism, deflecting the necessity for structural change through her tiny multi-racial body.

Via cute pictures of her posted on Kardashian's Instagram account and spread around the Internet, West is pressed into service of Kardashian's worldwide self-brand via the mobile and social technologies that make that brand maintenance possible. Indeed, she reconciles the tensions between exoticism and whiteness inherent to her mother's self-brand. The adorable baby is incorporated into the mother's brand, lending normalcy via motherhood to an extraordinary celebrity life. We see this, for example, in an image from Kardashian's Instagram in which she cradles North on her lap while being primped for a photo shoot. At the same time, of course, that added normalcy functions as part of Kardashian and her extended family's unique ability to profit from this type of reality performance.

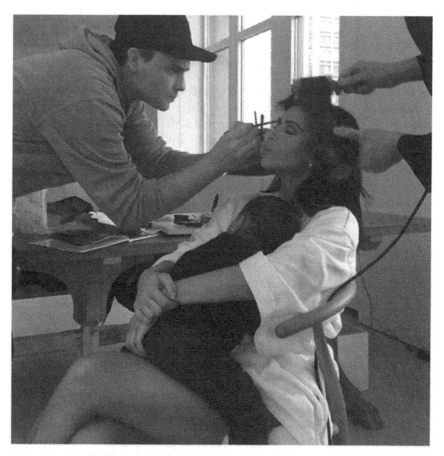

Figure 1.1 Kardashian cradles her daughter North West while being groomed for a photo shoot. Instagram https://www.instagram.com/p/y8GRLvOS_r/.

The baby Prince George is represented as a collective national baby, showcasing a plump-cheeked, blonde-haired, blue-eyed future Britain. Baby North West, in her mode as publicly adored social media toddler, represents a post-racial America. In this way, reality pregnancies and reality celebrity children embody a national brand that not only economically benefits the mother but also allows the audiences' affective reactions to the children to paint an idealized picture of valued multi-racial children that belies contemporary cultural and political realities of motherhood that disproportionately affect women of color and poor women.

Conclusions

Worldwide financial crisis began in 2007–08, and the US and the strongest European economies are only beginning to recover as of this writing in 2016. In 2011–14, we saw the highest number of anti-abortion laws proposed in US history. For both the US and Europe, recession has sparked a wave of immigration from poorer nations of people looking for work, accompanied by an influx of people fleeing violence and war. It is no accident that all of the fertility melodramas and at-risk pregnancies discussed in this chapter were represented in popular culture in this same period, and these are only a representative few. One could consider the birth of Kim Kardashian's nephews and niece, or her sister Khloe's frustrated desire for children; the reality program starring self-styled maternity concierge and "most fertile infertile person in the world," Rosie Pope, *Pregnant in Heels* (Bravo 2011–12); the infertility melodramas of plural wives on *My Five Wives* and *Sister Wives*; the constant tabloid speculation about Jennifer Anniston's womb; the list goes on and on.

Confronted with crisis, the heroic maternal (and her offspring) are asked to bear the ideological burden of representing the unspeakable or embodying irreconcilable cultural tensions. In the case of celebrities and reality personalities, those representations carry an even greater burden because they are linked to the real. While viewers understand the performativity of crafting a self-brand and perpetuating it on television, online, in consumer products, and magazines, these women are still portraying versions of themselves going about their daily family and work lives. What's more, authenticity and ordinariness are highly valued forms of contemporary celebrity, further blurring the line between reality and self-performance. Finally, their high production values, their stylishness, their network home, the affluence of the performers, the luxury (or even royalty) of the settings, all elevate these programs and performers above the common understanding of reality TV as trash. With that status, these women's heroic motherhood reinscribes the enormous value of wealthy white women's pregnancies. Those pregnancies benefit the individual woman's brand, making her a more effective neoliberal entrepreneurial subject, but they also make her a complete, happy postfeminist subject. These women's arduous journeys to this self-discovery result in their ample ability to care for themselves and their children, and even support their husbands. There is a near total absence of popular culture counter-narratives that might frame those immigrant women, poor women, and women of color victimized by anti-choice legislation, immigration restrictions, and financial crisis with no state support, as equally heroic mothers. Therefore, we are left with the impression that in a culture that values motherhood over all else, in fact, the only motherhood with real cultural and economic cachet is that of wealthy, white, entrepreneurial women. Nonetheless, even these women reveal challenges and even impossibilities in juggling postfeminist demands on their bodies, mommy culture's demands on their time and affective labor, and neoliberal and recessionary demands for their relentless brand expansion. These challenges, told in the feminized, open-ended, melodramatic mode, might offer a path toward embracing emergent feminisms, as I discuss in the concluding chapter.

Notes

1. "EW's 2015 Baby Power List," *Entertainment Weekly*, May 4, 2015. Available online at www.ew.com/article/2015/05/04/ew-baby-power-list-2015 (accessed April 8, 2016).
2. Lauren Berlant "America, 'Fat,' the Fetus," *boundary 2* 21.3 (Autumn 1994): 187.
3. Indeed there is a slew of scholarship about this cover. See Hilary Cunningham, "Prodigal bodies: Pop culture and Postpregnancy," *Michigan Quarterly Review* 41.3 (2002): 428–54; Robyn Longhurst, *Bodies: Exploring Fluid Boundaries* (London: Routledge, 2001); Carol Stabile, *Feminism and the Technological Fix* (Manchester: Manchester University Press, 1994); Imogen Tyler, "Skin-tight: Celebrity, Pregnancy and Subjectivity" in S.Ahmed and J. Stacey eds, *Thinking Through the Skin* (London: Routledge, 2001), 69–83.
4. The American slang MILF stands for mother I'd like to fuck. Jo Littler, "The Rise of the 'Yummy Mummy': Popular Conservatism and the Neoliberal Maternal in Contemporary British Culture," *Communication, Culture & Critique* 6 (2013): 227.
5. Kelly Oliver, *Knock Me Up, Knock Me Down: Images of Pregnancy in Hollywood Films* (New York: Columbia University Press, 2012), 2; Susan Douglas and Meredith Michaels, "Introduction," *The Mommy Myth: The Idealization of Motherhood and How It Has Undermined All Women* (New York: Free Press, 2004), Kindle Edition.
6. Clare Hanson, *A Cultural History of Pregnancy: Pregnancy, Medicine and Culture, 1750–2000* (Basingstoke, Hampshire, UK: Palgrave-MacMillan, 2004), 2.
7. Hanson, 37.
8. Hanson, 1–16.
9. Rebecca Kukla, *Mass Hysteria: Medicine, Culture, and Mothers' Bodies* (Lanham, Maryland: Rowman & Littlefield Publishers, 2005).
10. Rachel Cusk, *A Life's Work: On Becoming a Mother* (London: Fourth Estate, 2001).
11. Hanson, 1; "Protecting Your Personal Space," *Real Simple*, Undated; Lisa Mirza Grotts, "Belly Etiquette: To Touch or Not to Touch?" *Huffington Post*, July 18, 2012. Just a few examples of mommy blogs and magazines that discuss

the patting of pregnant bellies: Sara Jio, "10 Things I Didn't Know About Pregnancy," *Woman's Day*, Undated. Online; Michelle, "Pregnant Bellies Are Not Public Domain," *So Wonderful so Marvelous*, Personal Blog; "The Belly Pat," April 23, 2013, *A Day in the Life of a Semi-stressed Mom*, Personal Blog.

12. Jeffrey S. Passel, Gretchen Livingston, and D'Vera Cohn, "Explaining Why Minority Births Now Outnumber White Births," Pew Research Center, May 17, 2012. Available online at www.pewsocialtrends.org/2012/05/17/explaining-why-minority-births-now-outnumber-white-births/ (accessed April 8, 2016).

13. For detailed examples of the legal and political context, see this book's Introduction.

14. Alex Bevan, "The National Body, Women, and Mental Health in *Homeland*," in In Focus: Analyzing *Homeland*, Diane Negra and Jorie Lagerwey (eds.), *Cinema Journal*, 54.4 (August 2015).

15. Peter Brooks, *The Melodramatic Imagination* (New Haven: Yale University Press, 1976), 11.

16. Linda Williams, "Film Bodies: Gender, Genre, and Excess," *Film Quarterly* 44.4 (Summer 1991): 2–13.

17. Susan Bordo, *Unbearable Weight: Feminism, Western Culture, and the Body* (Berkeley: University of California Press, 1993).

18. For a discussion of reality TV's governmentality, see Laurie Ouelette and James Hay, *Better Living Through Reality TV* (Malden, MA: Blackwell Publishing, 2008).

19. Julie Wilson and Emily Yoachim coined the term "mamapreneur" to describe the way mothers facing economic precarity must become entrepreneurial to augment family incomes as well as ensure "their prosperity by rationalizing their everyday labours and emotions." Wilson and Yoachim's work is based on ethnographic interviews with non-celebrity "normal" women, but the concept applies to these celebrity women producing ideological content for viewer-consumers facing recession-era financial trouble, whether wealthy and famous or not. Wilson and Yoachim, "Mothering Through Precarity: Becoming Mamapreneurial," *Cultural Studies* 29.5–6 (2015): 669.

20. Shelley Cobb, "Mother of the Year: Kathy Hilton, Lynne Spears, Dina Lohan, and Bad Celebrity Motherhood," *Genders* 48 (2008): 3.

21. Bordo, 130.

22. Amanda Ann Klein, "Welfare Queen Redux: *Teen Mom,* Class and the Bad Mother" *Flow* 13.03 (November 12, 2010). Available online at http://flowtv.org/2010/11/welfare-queen-redux/ (accessed April 8, 2016).

23. Kirsten Pike, "'Birthin' Babies are Disgusting:' Women's Health in the *Honey Boo Boo* 'Apocalypse,'" *In Media Res*, Nov 5, 2012. Available online at http://mediacommons.futureofthebook.org/imr/2012/11/05/birthin-babies-are-disgusting-women-s-health-honey-boo-boo-apocalypse (accessed April 8, 2016).

24. Feuer, "'Quality' Reality and the Bravo Media Reality Series," *Camera Obscura* 88, 30.1 (2015): 190.

25. See for example, Tracie Egan Morrissey, "Can Rachel Zoe Get Pregnant?" *Jezebel* September 1, 2010 (accessed September 20, 2013); Amy L. Harper, "Exclusive! Rachel Zoe Wants a Baby, But experts Say She's Too Skinny to Get Pregnant," *Hollywood Life*, September 20, 2010 (accessed September 20, 2013).

26. "Zoe vs. Zoe," *The Rachel Zoe Project* 3.7, aired September 14, 2010.

27. "Fashion Addiction," *The Rachel Zoe Project* 3.8, Bravo, aired September 21, 2010.

28. Diane Negra, *What a Girl Wants: Fantasizing the Reclamation of Self in Post-feminism* (New York: Routledge, 2009).

29. "Zoe Couture: Styling the Stylist," *The Rachel Zoe Project* 5.8, Bravo aired April 24, 2013.

30. The TLC network's megafamilies, with upwards of a dozen children, are an exception to this rule. They are discussed in detail in Chapter Four.

31. Oliver, 178–9.

32. Oliver, 178.

33. Allison Corneau, "Giuliana Rancic: Duke's 2nd Birthday May Be at a Trampoline park," *Us Weekly* August 14, 2014. Available online at www.usmagazine.com/celebrity-moms/news/giuliana-rancic-duke-second-birthday-at-trampoline-park-2014148 (accessed April 8, 2016).

34. Oliver, 96; Sylvia Ann Hewlett, *Baby Hunger: The New Battle for Motherhood* (London: Atlantic Books, 2002).

35. *Us Weekly* cover. June 24, 2013.

36. Alice Leppert discusses Kim Kardashian's intense work ethic and 24/7 schedule in "Famous for the Fame-Work: *Keeping Up with the Kardashians* and the Production of Entrepreneurial Sisterhood," in *Cupcakes, Pinterest, and Ladyporn: Feminized Popular Culture in the Early Twenty-First Century*," Elana Levine, ed. (Urbana-Champaign: University of Illinois Press, 2015).

37. The term is used, for example, by feminist news and gossip cite Jezebel.com. Available online at http://jezebel.com/search?q=shinylocks (accessed October 15, 2013).

38. Jonathan Jones, "The Royal Baby Pictures Show Privilege Trying, and Failing, to Look Normal," Guardian.com, August 20, 2013 (accessed October 15, 2013).

39. See for example a *Star Magazine* cover that reads "Pregnancy and Anorexia Shocker! Kate 95lbs and Having a Baby!" July 25, 2011. Available online at thehollywoodgossip.com (accessed October 15, 2013); and Ed Riley, "Kate Middleton on Twitter Storm over Being 'Too Thin,'" *Daily Star* April 6, 2013 (accessed October 15, 2013).

40. Bonnie Rochman, "Is Kate Middleton Too Thin to Be Pregnant? It Isn't Easy Being Pregnant, and It Sure Isn't Easy Being a Pregnant Kate Middleton," *Time*, December 7, 2012 (accessed October 15, 2013).

41. "The Year in Us Weekly!" *Us Weekly* cover, October 10, 2011, accessed via "The Year in *Us Weekly!*" USmagazine.com (accessed October 15, 2013). Covers of *The Independent* and *The Daily Mail*, July 23, 2013 Via Max Fisher, "Here Are the Five Best British Tabloid Front Pages on the Royal Baby," *The Washington Post*, July 23, 2013 (accessed October 15, 2013).

42. Maria Pramaggiore and Diane Negra, "Keeping Up with the Aspirations: Commercial Family Values and the Kardashian brand," *Reality Gendervisions: Decoding Gender in Transatlantic Reality TV*, Brenda Weber, ed. (*Durham: Duke University Press, 2014).

43. Mary C. Beltrán, "The Hollywood Latina Body as Site of Social Struggle: Media Constructions of Stardom and Jennifer Lopez's 'Cross-Over Butt,'" *Quarterly Review of Film & Video* 19 (2002): 73, 72.

44. Pramaggiore and Negra, 86.

45. Cover, *Star*, April 15, 2013; Cover, *Star*, March 18, 2013; Cover, *Us Weekly*, April 1, 2013; Cover, *InTouch*, April 24, 2013. Available online at Intouch.com (accessed October 24, 2013).

46. Cover, *You*, May 9, 2013. Available online at You.co.za (accessed October 24, 2013).

47. See for example, "Kanye West Makes Kim Kardashian Throw Out All Her Clothes." *Us Weekly*, Usweekly.com, November 10, 2012 (accessed October 24, 2013); Cover, "Kim's Plan Backfires: Pregnant & Alone," *InTouchWeekly*, Hollywoodite.com (accessed October 24, 2013); "Dumped at 200 Lbs! and Other crazy Kardashian Headlines!" *Wetpaint*. Available online at www.wetpaint. com/dumped-at-200-lbs-and-other-crazy-kim-kardashian-headlines-770514/ (accessed April 19, 2016).

48. Anthony McIntyre, "Isn't She Adorkable!: Cuteness as Political Neutralization in the Star Text of Zooey Deschanel," *Television and New Media*, Online First Feb 28, 2014.

49. For an analysis of Angelina Jolie and Brad Pitt's celebrity family, see Diane Negra, "Brangelina: The Fertile Valley of Celebrity," *The Velvet Light Trap* 65 (Spring 2010): 60–61.

50. Jane Naomi Iwamura, "The Oriental Monk in American Popular Culture," in *Religion and Popular Culture in America*, Revised Edition, Bruce David Forbes and Jeffrey H. Mahan, eds. (Berkeley, CA: University of California Press, 2005), 32.

2 Bravo Brand Motherhood
Negotiating the Impossibilities of Postfeminism

During her first season appearing on *The Real Housewives of Atlanta* (2008–), Phaedra Parks was expecting her first child. Her pregnancy was not represented as difficult, uncomfortable, or risky for her health like Kim Kardashian's or Kate Middleton's pregnancies, described in the previous chapter. In fact, she flaunted her belly, her skin glowed, and she planned an outrageous baby shower for herself complete with hundreds of guests, cake, catering, gowns, roses in her hair, and rhinestones on her eyelids. The central celebration of motherhood and its demarcation as an event at least as important as marriage in defining a woman's identity, situates this moment, and the network brand it represents, firmly within the realm of postfeminist mommy culture described in the previous two chapters. The excess with which Phaedra celebrated herself and the eye rolling it inspired in her fellow cast members are emblematic of the Bravo network's winking address to middle-class consumers that simultaneously applauds and chastises its female stars for their embrace of postfeminist self-branding. This chapter examines the Bravo network brand and some of the performers on its flagship franchise, *The Real Housewives*. The US channel, a powerhouse of high production value "quality reality" television, fills the bulk of its programming lineup with affluent women ranging in age from their 20s to their 50s, all of them negotiating among performing authenticity, launching and promoting self-brands or other entrepreneurial endeavors, and structuring their identities around being wives and mothers. I argue that the network's tone, its relative diversity in casting, and the common generic trope of interspersing plot with confessional interviews, reveal the complexity of a culture reacting to recession but still invested in consumption; invested in postfeminist values but witnessing emerging feminisms. By focusing on "passion" and representing work as leisure, Bravo creates a popular, ratings-successful vision of postfeminist entrepreneurialism generally, and entrepreneurial motherhood more specifically. The network's tone and narrative structures, however, build in a critique that, I argue, consciously calls attention to the strictly enforced borders of successful postfeminist subjecthood. In so doing, Bravo and especially the *Real Housewives* franchise move from a vehicle for consumerist aspiration to a space of play, negotiated critique, and even a potential outlet for intersectional feminism masquerading as "trashy" reality TV.

Feminist media scholars in the US seem to have adopted Bravo as their network of choice for fandom as well as scholarship. It was Bravo, for example, that inspired Jane Feuer to coin the term "quality reality;" and its brand history, marketing strategies, production contexts, and political goals have all been the subject of scholarly analysis in addition to numerous representational analyses of its programming, particularly of its flagship franchise, *The Real Housewives* (2008–).[1] At first glance, Bravo's roster of mostly wealthy characters decorating homes, selling real estate, making dates for millionaires, or simply leading lives generally filled with lunches, galas, openings, and drinks seems far more appropriate for boom times than bust. Yet the network brand is rife with contradictions that release some of the tensions inherent in middle-class, recession-strapped audiences consuming seemingly celebratory shows about rich people. The exaggerated performances allow for mockery but also feature well-off women, many of whom fulfill the neoliberal mandate for entrepreneurialism, often struggling with the postfeminist binds of simultaneously being a deeply committed mother, a self-branded entrepreneur, and a hyper-feminine consuming subject. The feedback loop of confessional interviews, reunion shows, and network paratexts, including its own late night chat show, *Watch What Happens Live* (2009–), encourage laughter when these Bravo women fail to achieve the sought-after postfeminist ideal of perfect "balance." But the struggles, failures (and occasional successes), and playful humor of *The Real Housewives* and many of Bravo's other programs contain a remarkably diverse group of women in terms of age and race that gently criticizes regimes of white postfeminist motherhood and even personhood and, in the process, helps make those dominant structures visible. This chapter begins by exploring Bravo's brand identity, and in particular its distinctive tone and series of dualities. Focusing primarily on *The Real Housewives*, I examine how Bravo's multiplied mode of address creates layers of interpretable meaning that, due to their multiplicity, have the potential to challenge idealized images of pregnancy and motherhood, age and appropriate self-branding, economic hardship and work-life balance, and racial and regional diversity.

Bravo's Brand: "Winking" Postfeminism

Bravo was founded in 1980 as a television home for the performing arts and a decidedly high-culture take on film. Its original flagship program, *Inside the Actor's Studio*, an interview show featuring A-list Hollywood actors hosted by James Lipton, dean emeritus of the Actor's Studio Drama School, premiered in 1994. It still runs new episodes, but the rest of the network's identity has morphed over the years from arthouse film base to reality TV stable and one of the most lucrative non-sports channels on American cable television. Katherine Sender has detailed the network's rebranding, which she says kicked off with 2003's "summer of gay love." That summer, the channel premiered a "dualcasting" strategy targeting gay male and straight female audiences with the breakout hit *Queer Eye for the Straight Guy* (2003–07). Sender points out the risk Bravo took of diluting its formerly high-class brand with the low-brow reputation of reality TV. Bravo used gay performers, she argues, to tap into "their upscale associations, [helping] deflect the trashy shadow of reality television."[2] Bravo's high-gloss network-wide luxury aesthetic continues this pattern, deflecting the degraded status incurred by the soap opera conventions and feminized address of most of its programming. The melodramatic docusoap, *The Real Housewives*, is the heart of the female-targeted, gay friendly brand of playful, aspirational consumption, but Bravo offers an array of quality reality TV, including professional competition shows like *Top Chef* (2006–) and personality-driven workplace dramas like its *Million Dollar Listing* (2006–) franchise, or *Vanderpump Rules* (2013–).[3] In direct contrast to the surveillance camera style of reality TV stalwart *Big Brother* (CBS 2000–) and its copycats, or the intentionally degraded image of shows like *Jersey Shore* (MTV 2009–12), or its British twin *Geordie Shore* (MTV UK 2011–),[4] Bravo creates a polished, quality aesthetic that includes a bright color pallet, expensive big city locations, a frequent blend of wealthy, catty women, and always the knowing "Bravo wink."[5]

The "wink" is hard to define precisely, but it is essential to the network's tone and dual address, and is sometimes nearly a literal wink. The easiest place to pinpoint Bravo's tone is in the reaction shots in the direct address interview segments that interrupt, narrativize, and interpret onscreen events. In addition to offering explanations of the characters' motivations or background context to scenes, these reaction shots often create a conspiratorial or gossipy relationship between performer and viewer. They include an impressive array of silent looks, including blank, faux-uncomprehending stares like Rachel Zoe's, discussed in the previous chapter and perfected by *Real Housewife of Atlanta* NeNe Leakes. Another common reaction is the dismissive snort, a specialty of *Real Housewife of New York* Countess Luann de Lesseps, or the groans and eye rolls perfected by *Millionaire Matchmaker* Patti Stanger and *Real Housewife of Beverly Hills* Lisa Vanderpump. These reactions perform a knowingness and work to forge the affective bond between performer and viewer that is essential to self-branding. Of course, these judgmental reaction shots only maintain a character's superiority until she herself next acts out and is represented as too loud, too emotional, or excessive in her spending or undisciplined in her body. As with their daytime soap opera predecessors, identification shifts constantly, refusing ultimate judgment on any of the performers' actions.[6] This textual openness is compounded by Bravo's tone, which simultaneously promotes its performers, their products, and the luxurious lives they appear to lead, while conspiring with middle- and upper-middle-class consumers to mock and discipline their out-of-reach consumption and out-of-bounds behavior. This opportunity, as a viewer, to aspire to own a house in the luxury New York outpost of the Hamptons while simultaneously judging the frivolity of those who do is one of the unique pleasures of watching Bravo. As Stuart Hall describes it, the practice of this type of negotiated viewing necessarily involves comprehending the dominant and even seeing its appeal while also finding other, more hybrid ways to understand a text that speak more directly to a viewer's individual (non-dominant) subject position.[7]

In the same vein, Jane Feuer

> argues that melodrama ... produces two texts. The first or main text is that preferred by the dominant ideology, and is accessible at the superficial, 'obvious' level. The second text, however, is made available by the 'excess,' which overspills the control of the main text and subverts the dominant ideology.[8]

This duality (or multiplicity) of address repeats itself throughout the brand, creating a series of excesses and contradictions requiring interpretation that mirror the negotiation of contradictory and conflicting demands of postfeminist mommy culture. In one such contradiction, *The Real Housewives* is the "bad object" par excellence in popular culture. It is the go-to example used to dismiss feminized popular culture, used that way even by President Obama.[9] Yet, its target demographic of the relatively affluent, well-educated, pop culture savvy, liberal, urban-dwelling consumers are the same demographics likely to have been Obama supporters. This target viewer herself reflects the tensions between feminist achievement like education and professional success, and postfeminist disciplines over body, beauty, marriage, and parenting evident in Bravo's brand. Bravo still targets the audiences Sender noted, but the wink also manages to encapsulate the central paradox of postfeminism: Feminism has been accomplished and is no longer necessary, yet women "choose" to conform to the disciplinary norms of body shape, fashion, and emphasis on romance, mothering and care work that are central to postfeminist representation. This contradictoriness creates potential spaces of negotiated reading and feminist critique.

Bravo has labeled its target consumers "affluencers." "Affluencers" respond to the network's decidedly postfeminist "passion points" of food, fashion, beauty, design, digital and pop culture.[10] With its female centricity, emphasis on fashion, consumption, urban locations, and a feminized preoccupation with romance and motherhood, many Bravo shows are essentially versions of *Sex and the City*'s (HBO 1998–2004) "quality postfeminsim" come to life in the idiom of reality TV.[11] Indeed, the way avid viewers of high-brow, narratively complex, scripted drama might say they are fans of HBO rather than of an individual program, popular culture aficionados and "affluencers" might say they are fans of the entire Bravo network. Just as *Sex and the City* carved out a space within quality television discourse for a half-hour comedy about affluent, accomplished, hyper-feminine women's romantic and work lives during an economic boom, Bravo takes up that mantle during a period of recession and recovery that pushed always present inequalities of income, gender, and race back into the foreground of public discourse. The rest of this chapter analyzes individual Bravo programs and works to reveal the significance of the network's complex representations of motherhood as emblematic of a culture negotiating recession and recovery, postfeminism and reemerging feminism, and the heightened visibility of racial inequality in a supposedly postracial cultural moment. Bravo's open texture and the way so many of its shows revel in their performers' simultaneous success and failure at maintaining postfeminist ideals both release tension via humor and make those ideals more visible as ideological constructs. I begin by analyzing dominant readings of Bravo's postfeminist text, particularly the limits of wealth, age, and "proper" self-branding it enforces on its characters. I then shift to the negotiated readings made possible by Bravo's brand specificity and suggest that the network offers a more inclusive respite from those strict limits as well.

In keeping with the enormous cultural value placed on motherhood and celebrity in the early twenty-first century, Bravo consistently molds programs and creates "Bravolebrities" from affluent, entrepreneurial women whose relationship to motherhood is one of their defining characteristics. As of 2015, the *Housewives* had American versions in Atlanta, Beverly Hills, New York, Orange County, New Jersey, Miami, and Potomoc, Maryland (a wealthy suburb of Washington, DC), with international iterations in Cheshire, England and Melbourne, Australia. Many more of the network's past and present shows, like *Millionaire Matchmaker* (2008–), *Pregnant in Heels* (2011–12), *Untying the Knot* (2013–16), *Newlyweds: The First Year* (2012–), and even its first foray into scripted drama, *Girlfriend's Guide to Divorce* (2014–) feature women's dating, marital, and maternal status as the locus of identity and drama. These shows also frequently concentrate on stories of their stars building brands and businesses as in *Millionaire Matchmaker, Pregnant in Heels, Girlfriend's Guide*, and *The Rachel Zoe Project* (2008–13), further cementing the representational link between marriage, maternity, and self-branding and their perpetually essential role in achieving postfeminist adulthood.

Children and spouses are often structuring absences rather than central characters on Bravo shows, but the women at the center of its most popular franchise model postfeminist entrepreneurial motherhood in the same way that Erin Copple Smith argues Bravo performers model proper affluencer behavior.[12] *Real Housewives of New York*'s Bethenny Frankel is perhaps the most successful version of this, having not only created the Skinnygirl cocktail brand during her first stint on the show (she returned in 2015 after a divorce and the cancellation of her other attempts at television shows), but also parlayed her marriage, pregnancy, and young family into spinoff programs.[13] Rachel Zoe, whose incorporation of her children into her fashion brand is analyzed in Chapter One, is another stand out example, as is Heather Thomson, discussed below. Bravo's pervasive playful tone, however, frequently calls more attention to its performers' failures than their successes, creating layered texts that celebrate wealth, opulence, and female bickering while simultaneously recognizing essential challenges to those postfeminist norms.

Problematic Pregnancy

As we saw in the introduction, motherhood became embroiled in politics in the nineteenth century because reproduction was an issue of empire.[14] While empire has taken on different inflections in the twenty-first century—soft power, economic dominance, control over immigration, rather than direct colonization—the valorization of motherhood is still tightly linked to notions of empire that needed shoring up in the face of a struggling economy, failed, expanding, or never-ending wars abroad, and increasing or increasingly visible inequality on the basis of class and race. In such times of crisis, women's bodies are called into service as tools to promote and preserve the empire. Situating ever-increasing control over women's reproductive bodies and diminishing access to reproductive health care—common features of the twenty-first century US politics—within America's history of racial violence, including "slavery, Jim Crow, sterilization campaigns, the war on drugs," Steven Martinot argues that the "state's control of women's pregnant bodies has a strong racial component—black women's bodies are, and have always been, used in the United States as a mechanism to reconstitute the state as white."[15] The previous chapter's discussion of white women's heroic pregnancies illustrates that claim. I would argue, however, that Bravo actually offers a "quality" popular culture outlet where full adult subjectivity is available for women who do not fit the upper-middle-class, slender, white vision of motherhood exemplified on the *Time Magazine* cover that demanded "Are you mom enough?"[16] By creating reality melodramas with quite strictly segregated casts, Bravo offers a cultural and geographic specificity that denies claims to a "postracial" America and opens access to valorized motherhood to women who are not white. In the following two examples, a black woman in her 30s, Phaedra Parks, and a white woman in her 50s, Ramona Singer, illustrate the ways Bravo plays with the notion of the intensive mommy culture mother and what types of pregnancies are the most culturally valued. Both women either will not or cannot conform to the idealized maternal image, and both are made to seem foolish for not understanding that they are outside the limits of that ideal. Yet their excesses and misunderstandings are pleasurable, in part, because they throw into relief the ideal and its extremely narrow confines. The gently mocking affection Bravo cultivates for its stars lends an air of critique to that fetishized vision of mandated maternity.

Phaedra Parks's elaborate baby shower on *The Real Housewives of Atlanta* (*RHOA*) demonstrated both the importance of centralizing motherhood as the locus of postfeminist identity formation and revealed the unspoken boundaries of good taste within which that celebration of motherhood is intended to operate. Because pregnant bodies are a political discourse, Phaedra's blackness automatically racializes her supposedly gauche, excessive taste and doubles the ways in which she is represented as incorrectly performing expectant motherhood. That is, her baby shower is understood as crazy and over-the-top because she has unsophisticated nouveau riche "bad taste," but that bad taste is also linked to blackness. Contrast Phaedra's shower, for example, to the party Giuliana Rancic threw for her son's second birthday. Rancic's performance of white middle-class authenticity, as discussed in the previous chapter, demonstrates restraint and her husband's Midwestern "common sense" when she throws a smaller, family-only party. In contrast, Phaedra's spending is out of control and not mitigated by any of the elements that contain Rancic's celebration of her maternity. Phaedra's pregnancy takes on an additional note of the bizarre when, throughout the TV season, she does not seem to know when her baby is due. Mommy culture dictates certain elements of performance for the affluent, affect-intensive pregnancy it values most: replacing social media profile pictures with sonograms, posting monthly belly shots in profile, and meticulous knowledge of week-by-week fetal development and size in comparison to fruits and vegetables.[17] Phaedra refuses to participate in these rituals of time marking, obfuscating instead whenever asked how far along she is, conveniently creating a serialized dramatic arc for the show.

At a party just before the baby's birth, sole white castmate Kim Zolciak confronts Phaedra's friend (and baby shower planner) Dwight when he shares the happy news that Phaedra will give birth that week. "My whole thing," Kim asks, "is how far along is she? Why are they inducing this baby two months before?" Dwight's response, "Because he—he's developed," does not satisfy Kim, who reveals to everyone's surprise (voiced by cast member Cynthia Bailey's confessional segment) that before her reality TV career, she was a labor and delivery nurse. Kim responds: "She's having a f***ing alien then because it takes ten months to cook a baby."[18] Viewers are thus put in the unfamiliar position of turning to Kim, whose performance is usually focused on the bodily and behavioral excesses of her artificial hair and breasts, drinking alcohol and eating junk food, as the voice of reason. If *even* Kim understands Phaedra's pregnancy better than she does, the text seems to say, Parks is yet further outside the bounds of "correct" pregnancy than it seemed. This is only the most direct example of the cast challenging Phaedra's timeline, her intellectual understanding of pregnancy, and her emotional connection to her baby. As a result, Parks is represented as borderline unfit, and the excessiveness of her self-celebration, evidenced by the extravagant baby shower, is linked to an alienation from her own body and fetus. Phaedra's own statement, "I don't know about all that" when asked by her husband if she felt bonded to the fetus continues her characterization as outside the contemporary normative ideal of expectant motherhood. But Phaedra is not really represented as a villain (on *The Real Housewives*, unlike scripted soap operas, the only true marker of villainy is being boring). In the delivery room on the day of the birth, when Phaedra insists her baby is early and the doctor directly contradicts her on camera, it becomes clear that she has feigned her misunderstanding of biology to protect her mother, a Christian pastor, from the knowledge that the child was conceived before she was married. Castmate Kandi Burruss and the doctor share a laugh at Phaedra's bedside in the delivery room as the show cuts together silent reaction shots from Phaedra, her husband, and her mother, all seeming to carefully avoid eye contact with each other and the camera. Phaedra's self-celebratory excesses; her failed negotiation between the demands of good Christian daughter, reality performer, and pregnant woman within postfeminist mommy culture; and the comedy that results, particularly from the rest of the cast's reactions to her pregnancy, all exemplify Bravo's complex address and sardonic tone. More importantly, by showing nonconformity to that ideal and grounding that nonconformity with an explanation rooted in religious and family obligations—traditional American "family values" in keeping with the heightened value of motherhood—it makes the idealized performance more visible.

While pregnant, Phaedra might represent an "icon of excess," outside the bounds of the sacrificial image of a mother who commits her entire self to her child.[19] But after the birth, we see Phaedra breastfeeding and bathing her baby; in later seasons, she does the school run. We see her kneeling beside the bath or bedside wearing a baseball cap rather than the elaborate makeup and wardrobe she typically dons for on-camera appearances. Through all of these moments, the obvious love and care for her child, as well as her frank statements about her fear of motherhood and the boredom of caring for an infant, offer viewers a complex performance of authenticity that shores up Phaedra's "good" motherhood and gives "quality" audiences a rare representation of a black woman in the role of affluent, child-obsessed mother. In addition to incorporating affluent blackness into this white ideal, these moments offer a counter-narrative to the dominant version of postfeminist motherhood, showing the challenges, the lack of glamor, and the sharing of childcare among Phaedra, her husband, her mother, and paid care workers. Because children are often discussed, but remain infrequently seen on most of Bravo's shows, the scenes of Phaedra mothering her children (she has a second son in 2013) carry additional weight for being rare.

Age and Self-Branding

In addition to whiteness, another strictly delimiting element of the idealized postfeminist mother is age. She is typically in her thirties and can be neither too young nor too old. Phaedra fits within this age range, but *Real Housewife of New York*, Ramona Singer highlights postfeminism's constitutive "time panic." This obsession with time

> has forcefully renewed conservative social ideologies centering on the necessity of marriage for young women and the glorification of pregnancy; and ... has heightened the visibility of midlife women often cast as desperate to retain or recover their value as postfeminist subjects.[20]

Singer, an original cast member of *Real Housewives of New York (RHONY)*, is one of the oldest women in the Housewives franchise, a characteristic thrown into relief when the then-53-year-old believes she is pregnant.[21] She shares this confidence with the other cast members who, in their confessional segments, make it immediately clear that Ramona is nuts, that she is clearly going through menopause and mistaking the symptoms of aging for the symptoms of virility and pregnancy. This misreading of her own body on Ramona's part, like Phaedra's feigned misunderstanding of her pregnancy, is set up to make her look ridiculous, to distance her from her own reproductive body, the central site of postfeminist identity formation. The confessional segments make the viewer part of the conspiracy of mockery going on out of Ramona's immediate earshot. Yet Ramona's longevity despite numerous casting changes reveals her to be a fan favorite. In fact, her frequent performances of unruliness, perhaps best exemplified by her "crazy eyes," offer some of *RHONY*'s most consistent humor.[22] I argue that in repeatedly attempting and failing utterly to fit inside the harshly embodied limits of postfeminist entrepreneurial selfhood, she offers a refreshing respite from that ideal. Indeed, her affluent lifestyle and multiple businesses indicate a remarkable level of feminist achievement crafted while not fitting in to the demands for quietness, restraint, and domesticity. Because Bravo targets a well-educated, savvy viewer and cultivates multiple simultaneous readings of its texts, Ramona's success as a performer and entrepreneur would be visible to Bravo's "affluencers" despite—or perhaps because—it does not conform to postfeminist disciplinary norms.

It is not only this mistaken pregnancy that marks Singer's age and relative incomprehension of or nonconformity to the postfeminist ideals of female entrepreneurship. Early in season five, she meets new cast member Heather Thomson and the conflict between them becomes a season-long generational divide between Heather's expert navigation of the demands of postfeminist entrepreneurial motherhood and Singer's failure to find the correct balance among those demands. Thomson is founder and CEO of Yummie Tummie shapewear, a line of high-tech, girdle-like undergarments designed to squeeze and mold malleable soft bodies into smaller, smoother, more culturally desirable forms. She is characterized as a successful businesswoman and associates herself with the cultural cachet of celebrities like Jennifer Lopez and Sean Combs, which she demonstrates via personal snapshots taken when she worked for their fashion brands earlier in her career. Thomson clearly sees *RHONY* as a marketing opportunity for her self-brand, for Yummie, and for her work raising money and awareness for organ donation charities—an effort inspired by her own son's need for a liver transplant. Thomson is thus the ultimate postfeminist mom, a branding expert helping women achieve their best selves through body control and incorporating her son's illness into her self-brand.

During the first meeting between Thomson and Singer, Thomson smoothly navigates the porous boundaries between affective and paid labor, taking this scene as an opportunity to bolster her self-brand through sympathy as well as promote her commercial products. She tells the story of her young son's congenital health problems, describing in heart-wrenching detail how the child was near death in the days and weeks after he was born, which marks Heather as the perfect neoliberal, postfeminist subject. She is not only a mother, but a suffering mother, able, because of her business successes, to procure for her son the best doctors available and nurse him through his transplant and ongoing care. Like the difficult pregnancies discussed in Chapter One, her fraught maternity is rendered heroic, in large part, through her affect-laden performance and the accompanying implication that through the sheer force of her love, she was able to reshape her son's damaged body into a relatively healthy one. Her story, told in her office at the company she founded, encapsulates the incorporation of motherhood into a postfeminist self-brand and the erasure of any border between home life, affective labor, and work life. The past affective labor of caring for her son is repurposed into affective labor creating viewer sympathy and attachment in service of brand loyalty for her consumer products.

What makes this story noteworthy is Ramona's reaction. Having been on the show for five seasons at this point, Singer is certainly well aware that she is a convenient excuse to bring cameras to Thomson's workplace to facilitate promoting Yummie products. Despite her experience as a reality performer, however, Singer is taken aback by the intimacy of Thomson's story at what she understood was a business meeting. She responds by tearing up and telling her own story of suffering maternity, in which her daughter's umbilical cord was wrapped around her neck at birth, and for a terrible few minutes, it was unclear if her daughter would breathe and survive. The show then cuts to Thomson's to-camera confessional in which she characterizes Singer as self-centered and arrogant to turn a heartfelt revelation from Thomson into a story about herself—and, for Heather, a story that could not possibly measure up on the scale of pathos Heather herself has constructed. In Singer's confessional, she admits that she found Thomson's story totally inappropriate for the workplace, and while she was touched, she was unsure how to respond.

What sets off the subsequent bickering is the younger, celebrity-adjacent Thomson's characterization of Singer's response. In this misunderstanding, Singer ostensibly fails to read and respond to the situation correctly and fails to find the proper balance between performing affect-intensive motherhood and female entrepreneurship. Yet later in the same episode, we learn that Singer owned a financially successful business by the time she was 29 and that she set out to make her own money because her father "was not a nice guy." Ramona repeats this story more than once over the course of the series, framing it as a specifically feminist lesson taught her by her mother, and which she in turn teaches her own daughter. In postfeminism, however, "feminism is decisively aged and made to seem redundant," thus setting up Ramona's age as the instigating factor in a generation gap that paints Heather as the postfeminist who understands the contemporary brand economy and Ramona as the sometimes overtly feminist dinosaur who cannot quite keep up.[23]

In addition to being aged, Ramona is further excluded from the definitions of "correct" postfeminist success with her unruly behavior and the trashy consumer products she promotes. Where Heather's products help women control and contain their bodies and provide access to an extremely classed slender body ideal, Ramona's best known product is Ramona Pinot Grigio. While Bethenny Frankel's low-calorie Skinnygirl cocktails are painted as a smart innovation speaking to an under-served market and a body-conscious postfeminist market at that, Ramona's Ramona Pinot Grigio is painted as an offshoot of her possible alcoholism. Even her choice of a white wine rather than red seems less sophisticated, especially when coupled with her jewelry and skincare brands. The jewelry is costume and other cast members call it cheap. It shares the name True (it's called True Religion) with her skincare line, but each is spelled differently (True/Tru), has different colors, designs and logos; a clear missed opportunity for brand consistency represented at a future meeting with Heather as Ramona's failure to understand contemporary brand culture. Ramona Pinot Grigio, however, at least uses Ramona's name and capitalizes on her reality performance. Throughout *RHONY*, Ramona is demonstrated to be fond of her pinot, often appearing to be drunk at parties or demanding what is represented as an unsophisticated option at parties where it is not being offered. In these instances, Ramona's behavior is loud, aggressive, sometimes out of control, definitively not "within bounds" of postfeminist discipline.[24] And she has created a product line that offers access to that unruliness for her consumers. In other words, via her self-performance, she is translating her misunderstanding of the proper postfeminist boundaries on body and behavior to her unwitting consumers—not educating them to fit disciplined postfeminist boundaries like Heather's shapewear does, but encouraging "crazy" drunkenness. Again though, because Bravo trades in excess and unruliness, celebrating and denigrating its *Housewives* in equal measure, like Phaedra's pregnancy and early motherhood, Ramona offers an alternate vision of an adult female subjectivity outside the strict confines of postfeminist motherhood.

Balancing Recession and Excess

Because its performers' wealth is central to Bravo's brand, recession could have presented a particular challenge for the network's appeal. While the tone and structures of the network brand identity might critique the behavioral excesses that wealth apparently produces, it still creates affection for its stars and embeds class aspiration into all of its programming. Thus, the so-called Great Recession of 2007–08 and its long-lasting ramifications threatened a core tenet of the brand when it revealed the near impossibility of class aspiration. The network, however, actually incorporated financial struggles into some of its programming, easing some of the tension inherent in potentially struggling middle-class audiences watching rich performers display their luxury leisure-time activities. The first iteration of what would become Bravo's signature show, *The Real Housewives of Orange*

County (*RHOC*), premiered in 2006, riding a wave of reality shows based on scripted dramas that began when MTV premiered *Laguna Beach: The Real OC* (2004–06) to feed on the success of the scripted teen drama, *The OC* (CW 2003–07). *RHOC*, in turn, capitalized on the new national fascination with Orange County, one of the richest counties in the US, and the salacious soapiness of the scripted TV hit *The Desperate Housewives* (ABC 2007–12). *RHOC* spawned its first spin-off versions, *The Real Housewives of New York* and *The Real Housewives of Atlanta* in 2008, which meant that Bravo, already built on a foundation of aspirational consumerism, was investing in a franchise about ostentatious wealth just as the US and the rest of the world were headed toward financial disaster. Even amid recession and protest movements like Occupy that sought to shed light on growing income inequality, the *Housewives* franchise continued to expand and attract viewers, perhaps because it did not shy away from representing the consequences of recession for its casts. Over the course of the franchise history, at least twelve of the *Housewives* cast members have filed for bankruptcy, and many have been confronted with financial insecurity onscreen in various other ways.[25] As Vicki Mayer notes, one Orange County *Housewife* was even forced "to (shock) go back to work" outside the home.[26] Furthermore, because reality performance is always spread across TV text, publicity materials, and tabloid culture, rumors constantly circulate about *Housewives'* potential financial troubles and the likelihood that their lifestyles are all a façade to begin with. Alternatively, during and after the recession, Bravo framed financial hardship as a chance to rebrand oneself. For example, another Bravolebrity, Jeff Lewis, who created his brand by flipping real estate on *Flipping Out* (2007–), had to downgrade to interior design when the housing bubble burst, eventually parlaying his financial troubles into a branding opportunity, and spinning off a new show *Interior Therapy with Jeff Lewis* (2012–13) in which he both renovated clients' homes and guided them through amateur couples' therapy.

Bravo's dual address, encouraging luxury consumption while mocking its own performers when they indulge in that consumption to excess, releases some of the tension inherent in celebrating upper-class wealth for middle-class viewers, especially in a recession era. But, in a move similar to the narrative that reframes intensive motherhood and domesticity as voluntary, nostalgic retreats rather than economic necessities, Bravo's brand also reframes the ideological power of the female stars whose self-brands it helps promote and create, from feminist achievement to post-feminist branding. So Heather's Yummie success is textually tied to the stories she tells in her office—stories of celebrity and motherhood, not training, financial outlay, long hours or any other aspect of typically masculinized paid work. Another pleasure of watching the *Housewives* is the humor created when some performers understand that entrepreneurialism and self-branding are culturally valued in the face of economic precarity, but then nonetheless make the "wrong" choices about how to do it. New

York *Housewife* Sonja Morgan, for example, faces bankruptcy after going through a divorce; yet she misreads viewers' class aspirations when she attempts to launch a line of designer toaster ovens. Rather than offering consumers an affordable version of something glamorous, or a product to help them achieve ideals of postfeminist beauty (like the slender but fun body implied by the likes of Yummie, Skinnygirl, or Kandi Burruss's line of sex toys, Bedroom Kandi), she offers them simple, low-cost, "trashy" cooking that one could as easily achieve in a college dorm room as in a fabulous New York kitchen. The ironic promotional photo shoot of Sonja draped in couture gowns and designer jewels while putting meals in a countertop oven seemed tailor made for Bravo's winking tone, but failed to hit the right balance between aspiration and authenticity, and the product never launched.[27] Like Ramona Singer's multiple products with different logos dispersed the value of her name recognition rather than consolidating it under one coherent brand identity, so Morgan's first attempt at self-branded entrepreneurialism failed to find the right postfeminist "balance" between domesticity and aspiration.

The importance of balance, i.e. treading precisely the right path between the feminist achievement of successful paid work and hiding that work via the visible trappings of postfeminism and the affective labor of brand management and self-performance, echoes another central postfeminist "balance" between work life and home life. Bravo shows often emphasize the blurriness of lines between home and work in contemporary brand culture. Morgan's toaster oven photos, for example, are taken in her Manhattan home, and Jeff Lewis lives in the houses he renovates on *Flipping Out*. Indeed, excepting *Top Chef*, nearly all of Bravo's programming takes place within the (supposedly) daily routines and domestic spaces of its performers. *Housewives* visit each other for lunch or a party; real estate programming shows agents at work in the domestic spaces they are selling; and even the stars' offices are often in their homes. To demonstrate how essential this notion of balance is to Bravo's brand and how delicate a balance it must be, I analyze a show that failed to find the balance and consequently lasted only ten episodes. *Kell on Earth* followed Kelly Cutrone, founder of bi-coastal fashion PR firm People's Revolution.[28] The business was run, and the program was filmed, in Cutrone's Manhattan brownstone, and the company's focus on fashion branding seems a perfect fit for the luxury postfeminist motherhood that constitutes so much of the Bravo reality TV schedule. Further solidifying her as an apparently solid fit for Bravo's brand, Cutrone penned two self-help books (one while filming the show) called *If You Have To Cry Go Outside: And Other Things Your Mom Never Told You* and *Normal Gets You Nowhere* that were targeted at young women learning to navigate the boundaries between business success and "appropriate" performances of femininity.[29]

Cutrone's fashion-centric business, captured at its most chaotic in the weeks leading up to and during Fashion Weeks in New York, Los Angeles, and London, hits three of its network's five "passion groups" with fashion, beauty, and pop culture. Shot in 2010, it shows Cutrone and People's Revolution also tapping into the digital culture passion point while learning to navigate (for them) new waters of transmedia marketing. *Kell* repeats Bravo's formula of following female entrepreneurs about their work and family lives. Cutrone's house, a So-Ho row house with living spaces on the 4th floor and the People's Revolution offices below, allows her to spend time with 7-year-old daughter Ava without sacrificing her extraordinarily long working hours. More importantly for Bravo, it condenses work and life spaces into a single shooting location, making its patented conflation of home and work life more convenient for production, and potentially highlighting the ease of constructing the work/life balance so important to postfeminist subjectivity.

The show is shot primarily in Cutrone's office, which is messy, crowded, and nearly entirely black and white, a direct contrast to Bravo's typically sun-kissed, color-saturated domestic and leisure spaces. The emphasis on the geography of urban centers, luxury tourism, and notably, sunshine, in LA, Atlanta, Orange County, Miami, the Hamptons, and Manhattan in the summer (the shooting locations of most *Housewives* shows and, indeed, almost all of Bravo's programming), is absent from Cutrone's 20-hour work day existence. The low-rent aesthetic (thought not fact) of both the office décor and the shooting style, in comparison to the rest of Bravo's reality stable, reveals fashion and branding to be hard work. In contrast, for example, the economic labor of creating and marketing Skinnygirl is de-emphasized on *The Real Housewives of New York* in favor of focusing on the overwrought emotional labor of Frankel's relationships with boyfriend (subsequently, husband and ex-husband) Jason Hoppy, her estranged father, and her (now former) best friend and castmate Jill Zarin.[30] The self-as-brand nature of Frankel and other Bravo stars' business ventures means that there is a constant performance of self, a calculated discipline over bodies, dress, weight, makeup, and relationships.

Cutrone, in contrast, is in the business of promoting other people, making self-promotion and self-branding explicitly forbidden. Any People's Revolution employee working an outside event must wear all black, the better to fade into the background and not draw attention away from the real commodity, the clothes and the personalities there to wear, advertise, and purchase the fashion. In other words, Cutrone's business, seemingly perfect for the self-as-commodity, female- and fashion-centric Bravo brand, commits the cardinal sin of pointing out ways in which self-branding is detrimental to her actual business. This unwillingness to mask paid work with the affective labor of self-branding calls too much attention to the disjunctures between feminist and postfeminist achievement. Cutrone's flat, affectless (or professional) demeanor and disheveled (for Bravo) appearance puts the feminist achievement of her paid work front and center in the text itself, unmasked by the typically Bravo excesses of wardrobe, makeup and performance. In other words, *Kell* disrupts the negotiated reading practices of savvy Bravo consumers by taking away the wink and putting the contradictions of postfeminism in the text itself, instead of the subtext.

For example, while running a profitable business might be labeled a feminist achievement, being a doting mother characterizes postfeminist success. One of Bravo's brand images is that of a luxury version of labor-intensive postfeminist motherhood, but while Cutrone's nanny is not featured, she is not hidden. Cutrone's constant worry about her limited time with daughter Ava calls attention to the extreme difficulty of accomplishing both the affective labor of motherhood and the economic labor of owning a business with the casual ease and implied lack of paid help seen so often on other shows. Cutrone's mothering is actively displaced onto her staff as she talks about "raising" rather than training her employees, fixes them up on dates, and frequently refers to herself as their mother figure and "Momma Wolf." This displacement of affect from biological daughter to employees and further to the book-buying public (the subtitle of her career advice book, after all, is *And Other Things Your Mother Never Told You*) further highlights the value placed on maternalism, but it also emphasizes how little actual mothering of her own child Cutrone is able to do while running her business. The impossibility of containing these contradictions is further evidenced in Cutrone's near constant discussion of the economic recession and its threat to her business. For its brief ten episodes, *Kell on Earth* illustrated the ideological contradictions of Bravo's style of luxury postfeminism. On one level, a woman who openly says she does not fit in, does not wear makeup, and never buys the clothes she promotes obviously is not a suitable brand ambassador for a company like Bravo that is built on selling affordable luxury and benefitting directly from advertising dollars paid by cosmetics and clothing companies. Cutrone's critique was too overt, Cutrone herself was too earnest, and the show's focus was too much on work rather than leisure. But Cutrone's very failure in this regard makes visible the precision with which Bravo calibrates its multiple levels of address, revealing oppressive cultural norms with gentle critique necessarily masked by humor and play.

Race and Regionalism

Reflecting its efforts to appeal to the widest possible range of upscale viewers as well as another challenge to the dominant whiteness of fetishized postfeminist motherhood, Bravo features an impressively diverse array of female performers from a wide range of ages, races, ethnicities, and regions, even though dating, marriage, and motherhood are typically key persona-defining characteristics for all of them. This diversity illustrates the pervasive nature of the disciplinary aspects of mommy culture, but it also presents the image of idealized maternity described in the opening of this book, as well as the cultural value it brings to women of color who perform themselves with regional and racial specificity.

Bravo's programming is carefully geographically specific and strictly segregated. *The Real Housewives of Miami* (2011–), for example, features an all Latina cast, while the *Shahs of Sunset* (2012–) is set in Los Angeles's Persian community. *Blood, Sweat & Heels* (2014–) features an all-black cast of professional women in New York City, younger than their white counterparts on *RHONY*. The network even occasionally reveals the unspoken normativity or supposed racelessness of whiteness. The white cast of *Real Housewives of New Jersey* (2009–), for example, is definitively ethnically marked as Italian American. In another example, in 2014, Bravo premiered *Southern Charm* (2014–), a docusoap following a group of rich, twenty-something, white men and women in Charleston, South Carolina with a promotional poster featuring the cast, clad entirely in white, on a plantation style porch painted entirely white. The only hint of color on the page came from some trees well in the background, creating a bright but low contrast almost monochrome image that gave the impression of pale Caucasian skin tones blending into the bleach white color of blank paper, with just a hint of a rural location coloring the background. When the image appeared in New York City subways, they were immediately graffitied with slogans like "white power" and "nazi shit."[31] Of course, this bad publicity is extratextual, yet the almost aggressive amount of white space on the original image, and the show's setting in a Southern capital city known for its beautifully preserved nineteenth century homes and its prominent role in the slave trade, reveal an investment in whiteness and make the too-often invisible dominance of whiteness visible through precisely the negotiated and oppositional viewing practices the network cultivates. *Southern Charm*, set in the same brand and potentially the same televisual flow as other geographically specific and ethnically or racially segregated programming, presents whiteness as a geographically and racially specific entity as well. In this way, whiteness, often powerful via its invisibility and presumed "normalcy" is revealed as a racialized category, offering a (admittedly limited) challenge to the unspoken dominance of whiteness in American popular culture. The segregation across the majority of its hit shows might seem to make Bravo's particular vision of postfeminist economic success something available only to upper-class white women who are willing to commit themselves to the extreme body discipline and the limited range of industries that fit in the network's "passion points."[32] I argue, on the contrary, that this segregation belies the whitewashing common when performers of color are cast in programs that ostensibly do not deal with race. Instead, it offers a range of postfeminist entrepreneurial mothers that extends far beyond the normally enforced rules of age and race and, within the larger brand identity of the network, offers a vision of intersectionality, if not overt feminism.

The Real Housewives of Atlanta (*RHOA*), with an almost entirely black cast, is consistently one of the network's highest-rated shows, and, indeed, it is one of the most watched shows in its timeslot.[33] In early seasons, its stars divided themselves between the Talls and the Smalls, but the show did, in fact, offer a wider range of embodied femininity than its white cast counter-parts. On the one hand, the cast features NeNe Leakes's tall, imposing figure alongside the extremely slender body of model Cynthia Bailey, the compact, athletic Kandi Burruss, the curvier DeShawn Snow, Kim Zolciak-Bierman's unruly and artificial white body, and muscular Sheree Whitfield, who favors intense boxing workouts that build muscle rather than focus on reducing body mass as is so often the case with workouts marketed toward women. On the other hand, the Atlanta women's bodies are represented as sites of labor, available for intervention in ways that the white New York women's disciplined and contained postfeminist bodies are not. The women in every *Housewives* city have surely sunk small fortunes into beauty maintenance and anti-aging regimens, but we see those interventions onscreen only infre-quently and then as cites of leisure—a trip to the nail salon for conversation in New York, for example. The Yummie and Skinnygirl brands are textual evidence that body work is part of these women's lives; however, for them, it is more often a matter solved with consumer products simultaneously pro-moting the women's own brands. For the Atlanta women, body shaping is a matter for intense physical labor like Sheree's boxing, or expensive, painful, invasive surgical intervention for NeNe and Kim. But it lacks the celebration of consumption that we see, for example, when *Real Housewives of Beverly Hills*'s Adrienne Malouf throws a spa party promoting Botox, and without exploiting the opportunity for furthering their own selves-as-brands outside the confines of the show.

By making the need for more physical intervention and labor visible within the show, *RHOA* in some ways demonstrates black bodies as in need of more work than the white bodies to achieve the disciplined, "success-ful" postfeminist maternal body. This portrayal reproduces old stereotypes of black embodiment versus white intellectualism and, set in contrast to the successful consumer product companies so evident on the New York franchise, highlights a comparative failure to exploit the opportunity for product creation offered by the show. This simple dichotomy, along with the racial segregation Bravo practices with most of its shows, is complicated by Bravo's winking brand identity and NeNe's status as one of the network's most loved stars. Rather than reinforcing the segregated vision of successful postfeminist subjectivity, the labor-intensive and surgically enhanced bodies of *RHOA* expose the narrowly defined access to the aspirational ideal rep-resented by the other texts analyzed in this book. Comparing *The Bachelor*'s (ABC 2002–Present) mostly white representations of game show dating to *Flavor of Love*'s (Vh1 2006–08) mostly black cast of essentially the same format, Kristen Warner concludes that *Flavor* "embodied the instability of whiteness through its many ruptures in ideologies of marriage, of capitalist consumption, and of femininity."[34] Warner argues that whiteness includes the high cultural value normatively placed on marriage, capitalist consump-tion (to which I would add entrepreneurialism), and femininity. *Flavor*'s over-the-top scenarios and performances, alongside star Flavor Flav's self-aware performance, has much in common with Bravo's layered, winking tone. *RHOA* similarly highlights the ruptures in Bravo's brand of postfeminist discipline and entrepreneurialism and moves the show from a vehicle for consumerist aspiration to an example of successful brand-selves emerging outside the strict limits of postfeminist entrepreneurial success set by Bravo's other stars. *RHOA* thus actually opens that definition of success to other (affluent) populations. Rather than "blindcasting" that Warner points out often results in whitewashing or subsuming racial or cultural specificity into dominant white norms, the *Housewives* regional, racial, and ethnic separation encourages performative specificity to differentiate one cast from another within the franchise.[35] Bravo's carefully segregated programming does not offer the postracial utopia hinted at through Kim Kardashian's pregnancy and young family discussed in Chapter One. Instead, Bravo attempts to reach a wider swath of its core demographic by understanding "affluencers" as a classed, but not racialized, category. Racialized reality TV performances and, in particular, representations and performances of African American women on reality docusoaps have been the subject of much analysis.[36] A common theme among some of this scholarship is the constant embrace of excess in these shows that, like all melodramatic excess, allows for meaning to be created in that which overspills the strict boundaries of text, good taste, and in this context, the enthroned, white image of ideal motherhood. Racquel Gates writes specifically about "unapologetically trashy reality" shows like *Love and Hip Hop* (VH1 2010–) and *Basketball Wives* (VH1 2010–), in contrast to the "quality reality" label Jane Feuer has associated with Bravo; however, Bravo's quality status only strengthens her argument when applied to *RHOA*.[37] She argues that,

> the reason that the women on *Basketball Wives* cling so tightly to their "wife" status is because black women have usually been excluded from an understanding of what it means to be one. Historically, the characteristics associated with the very image of a "wife" (white, middle class, appropriately feminine) have been defined in contrast to the lived experiences of black women, and often used to exclude them from the social, political, and financial privileges associated with its status.[38]

I would argue that in addition to more accurately reflecting a much wider cross-section of American motherhood than Rachel Zoe or Giuliana Rancic, *The Real Housewives of Atlanta* offers a version of motherhood that is entrepreneurial and self-branded—the requirements of postfeminist mommy culture—but rejects its whiteness while offering a mode of motherhood (they're *Housewives* just like everyone else) that acknowledges the near impossibility of attaining the "perfect mom" mold.

Bravo is hardly a socialist, intersectional feminist utopia challenging the dominant cabal of whiteness, neoliberal brand capitalism, and the overvaluing of a single, narrowly defined mode of motherhood. Indeed, its consistent representations of wealth and its address to affluent, savvy, educated consumers suggests precisely the opposite: It represents the most culturally valued forms of motherhood, branding, and entrepreneurialism. Yet its doubled structures, the brand-specific tone of its cast interviews, and its performers' self-awareness create excesses that offer or even demand a critical reading of that dominant. Its simultaneous love and scorn for its performers reveals the negotiated complexity of a culture reacting to recession, but still targeting aspirational consumers; the geographical and racial specificity of its casts speak to the relatively recent surge in mainstream visibility of racial inequality in the US. All of its wealthy, high-achieving female performers, operating within the *Housewives* brand identity, reveal some of the conflicting limits and demands of postfeminism and an emerging elite feminism.

Notes

1. Jane Feuer, "'Quality' Reality and the Bravo Media Reality Series," *Camera Obscura* 30.1 (2015): 185–95. See also Katherine Sender, "Dualcasting: Bravo's Gay Programming and the Quest for Women Audiences," *Cable Visions: Television Beyond Broadcasting*, Sarah Banet-Weiser, Cynthia Chris, Anthony Freitas, eds. (New York: New York University Press, 2007), 302–18; Erin Copple Smith, "'Affluencers' by Bravo: Defining an Audience Through Cross-Promotion," *Popular Communication* 10(4) 2012: 286–301; Pier Dominguez, "'I'm Very Rich, Bitch!': The Melodramatic Money Shot and the Excess of Racialized Gendered Affect in the *Real Housewives* Docusoaps," *Camera Obscura* 88, 30.1 (2015): 155–83; Kristen J. Warner, "'They Gon' Think You Loud Regardless: Ratchetness, Reality Television, and Black Womanhood," *Camera Obscura* 88, 30.1 (2015): 129–53; and Julia Himberg, in press.
2. Katherine Sender, "Dualcasting: Bravo's Gay Programming and the Quest for Women Audiences," *Cable Visions: Television Beyond Broadcasting*, eds. Sarah Banet-Weiser, Cynthia Chris, Anthony Freitas, (New York: New York University Press, 2007), 313.
3. *Million Dollar Listing* follows the professional and personal lives of high end real estate brokers. It is an opportunity to ogle ostentatiously expensive homes in New York, Los Angeles, and Miami, with some personal drama between competing realtors thrown in. *Vanderpump Rules*, a spin-off of *The Real Housewives of Beverly Hills* features the relationship dramas of the young, beautiful, sexually active staff at Housewife Lisa Vanderpump's West Hollywood restaurant Sur.
4. See Amanda Ann Klein, "*The Hills, Jersey Shore*, and the Aesthetics of Class," *Flow TV* 13.12. Available online at http://flowtv.org/2011/04/the-hills-jersey-shore-and-the-aesthetics-of-class/ (accessed January 21, 2016).
5. Emma Rosenblum, "The Natural: How Andy Cohen Became Bravo's Face," *New York Magazine*, January 8, 2010 (accessed May 29, 2013).
6. See Tania Modeleski, "The Search for Tomorrow in Today's Soap Opera," in *Feminist Television Criticism*, Charlotte Brunsdon, Julie D'Acci, and Lynn Spigel, eds. (Oxford: Oxford University Press, 1997), 36–47.
7. Stuart Hall, "Encoding, Decoding," in *The Cultural Studies Reader*, ed. Simon During, (London: Routledge, 1993), 90–103.

8. Quoted in John Fiske, *Television Culture*, (New York: Routledge, 1989), 192.

9. Racquel Gates, "Activating the Negative Image," *Television and New Media* 16.7 (2015): 616–30; Kristen J. Warner, "'They Gon' Think You Loud Regardless: Ratchetness, Reality Television, And Black Womanhood," *Camera Obscura* 88, 30.1 (2015): 129–53.

10. Available online at www.Affluencers.com, Bravo's ad sales website (accessed May 29, 2013). For a discussion of affluencers, see Erin Copple Smith, "'Affluencers' by Bravo: Defining an Audience Through Cross-Promotion," *Popular Communication* 10.4 (2012): 286–301.

11. Diane Negra, "Quality Postfeminism?: Sex and the Single Girl on HBO," *Genders* 39 (2004). Available online at www.iiav.nl/ezines/IAV_606661/IAV_606661_2010_52/g39_negra.html (accessed January 31, 2016).

12. Smith cites stars like Patti Stanger of *Millionaire Matchmaker*, Gail Simmons, a judge on *Top Chef*, as well as the *Housewives* as on air talent who embody the upscale, well-educated, trend-influencing target Bravo acolyte. Erin Copple Smith, "'Affluencers' by Bravo: Defining an Audience Through Cross-Promotion," *Popular Communication: The International Journal of Media and Culture* 10(4) 2012: 286–301.

13. See Suzanne Leonard and Diane Negra, "After Ever After: Bethenny Frankel, Self-Branding, and the 'New Intimacy of Work,'" in *Cupcakes, Pinterest, and Ladyporn: Feminized Popular Culture in the Early Twenty-First Century*, ed. Elana Levine (Urbana: University of Illinois Press, 2015).

14. Clare Hanson, *A Cultural History of Pregnancy: Pregnancy, Medicine and Culture, 1750–2000* (New York: Palgrave-MacMillan, 2004), 83.

15. Steven Martinot, "Motherhood and the Invention of Race," *Hypatia* 22.2 (Spring 2007): 80.

16. Kate Pickert, "The Man Who Remade Motherhood," *Time Magazine*, May 12, 2012.

17. According to whattoexpect.com, the online community version of the best-selling pregnancy advice book *What to Expect When You're Expecting*, now in its fourth edition, fingernails begin to grow in week 12, for example. According to the popular US parenting magazine *Parents*, at week 10 a fetus is the size of a kumquat. Heather Morgan Shott, "How Big Is Your Baby This Week?" *Parents*, undated. Available online at www.parents.com/pregnancy/week-by-week/how-big-is-your-baby-this-week/#page=9 (accessed April 9, 2016); "Week by Week Pregnancy Calendar," whattoexpect.com, undated.

18. "Is There a Doctor in the House?" *The Real Housewives of Atlanta* 3.08, aired November 21, 2010.

19. Diane Negra and Yvonne Tasker use this phrase to describe the way postfeminist consuming women are represented in recession-era popular culture. Negra and Tasker, "Introduction: Gender and Recessionary Culture," *Gendering the Recession: Media and Culture in an Age of Austerity*, Negra and Tasker, eds. (Durham, NC: Duke University Press, 2014), 4.

20. Diane Negra, *What A Girl Wants? Fantasizing the Reclamation of Self in Postfeminism* (New York: Routledge, 2009), 47.

21. "L.O.V.E. duel," *Real Housewives of New York* 4.16, Bravo, aired July 21, 2011.

22. "Crazy eyes" is the name given to Ramona's signature facial expression in which her eyes are open so wide that an enormous amount of white is visible above her

brown irises. The genuinely unusual look is akin to a "deer in the headlights" stare and gives the impression of simultaneous vacancy and extreme excitement. Coupled with Singer's blond hair and often bewildered reactions to news delivered onscreen, the look gives an impression of ditziness and is perhaps the most frequently seen incarnation of her unruly or not-strictly-disciplined-enough behavior.

23. Angela McRobbie, "Post-feminism and Popular Culture" in *Media Studies: A Reader*, 3rd ed., eds. Sue Thornham, Caroline Bassett, and Paul Marris. (New York: New York University Press, 2009), 350.
24. Diane Negra, *What a Girl Wants? Fantasizing the Reclamation of Self in Post-feminism*. (New York: Routledge, 2009), 139.
25. Youyoung Lee and Liat Kornowski, "*The Real Housewives* of Bankruptcies, Businesses and Divorces by the Numbers," *Huffington Post*, January 25, 2013.
26. Vicki Mayer, "Housewives in Crisis, Economic That Is," *Antenna: Responses to Media and Culture*, January 23, 2010. Available online at http://blog.commarts.wisc.edu/2010/01/23/housewives-in-crisis-economic-that-is/ (accessed October 28, 2013).
27. In 2015, Morgan launched Sonja Morgan New York, a fashion brand with the tagline "Every woman deserves luxury." The online brand's minimalist design and high prices make it a better fit for the aspirational consumerism Bravo endorses. Available online at www.sonjamorgannewyork.com/dresses/ (accessed January 31, 2016).
28. An earlier version of this section first appeared at Flowtv.org: "*Kell on Earth*: Kelly Cutrone and the Rare Failure of Brand Bravo," *Flow TV* 18.1 (June 20, 2013). Available online at http://flowtv.org/2013/06/kell-on-earth/ (accessed April 9, 2016).
29. Kelly Cutrone with Meredith Bryan, *If You Have to Cry, Go Outside: And Other Things Your Mother Never Told You*. (New York: Harper Collins, 2010); Kelly Cutrone with Meredith Bryan, *Normal Gets You Nowhere*. (New York: Harper Collins, 2011).
30. See Suzanne Leonard and Diane Negra, "After Ever After: Bethenny Frankel, Self-Branding, and the 'New Intimacy of Work,'" in *Cupcakes, Pinterest, and Ladyporn: Feminized Popular Culture in the Early Twenty-First Century*, Elana Levine, ed. (Urbana: University of Illinois Press, 2015).
31. "These Bravo Ads Are Pretty Racist, Right? Right," *Brooklyn Magazine*, February 7, 2014. Available online at www.bkmag.com/tag/bravo/ (accessed February 19, 2016).
32. Bravo's Ad Sales Website Lays Out Its Brand Profile and Its Audience's "Passion Points." Available online at www.affluencers.com/ (accessed May 29, 2013).
33. Maria Valiente, "*Real Housewives of Atlanta* Beats All of NBC's Scripted Programs in Ratings." Available online at www.wetpaint.com/real-housewives-of-atlanta/articles/real-housewives-of-atlanta-beats-all-of-nbcs-scripted-programs-in-ratings.
34. Kristen J. Warner, "'Who Gon' Check Me Boo': Reality TV as haven for Black Women's Affect," *Flow TV* 14.6. Available online at http://flowtv.org/2011/08/who-gon-check-me-boo/ (accessed January 18, 2016).
35. Kristen J. Warner, "The Racial Logic of *Grey's Anatomy*: Shonda Rhimes and Her 'Post-Civil Rights, Post-Feminist' Series," *Television and New Media* 16.7 (November 2015): 633.

36. See, for example, Pier Dominguez, "'I'm Very Rich, Bitch!': The Melodramatic Money Shot and the Excess of Racialized Gendered Affect in the *Real Housewives* Docusoaps," *Camera Obscura* 88, 30.1 (2015): 155–83; Racquel Gates, "Activating the Negative Image," *Television and New Media* 16.7 (2015): 616–630; Kristen J. Warner, "'They Gon' Think You Loud Regardless: Ratchetness, Reality Television, and Black Womanhood," *Camera Obscura* 88, 30.1 (2015): 129–53; Kristen J. Warner, "'Who Gon' Check Me Boo': reality TV as Haven for Black Women's Affect," *Flow TV* 14.6. Available online at http://flowtv.org/2011/08/who-gon-check-me-boo/ (accessed January 18, 2016).

37. Gates, "Activating the Negative Image."

38. Racquel Gates, "You Can't Turn A Ho into a Housewife: *Basketball Wives* and the Politics of Wifedom," *In Media Res*, September 26, 2011. Available online at http://mediacommons.futureofthebook.org/imr/2011/09/26/you-cant-turn-ho-housewife-basketball-wives-and-politics-wifedom (accessed January 18, 2016).

3 From Honest to GOOP
Lifestyle Brands and Celebrity Motherhood

Between 2008 and 2015, a slew of film and television actresses launched lifestyle brands to supplement or, to a certain extent, replace their entertainment industry work. Some of these women, like Jessica Alba, have framed their decisions as stemming explicitly from motherhood. Oscar-winning actress Gwyneth Paltrow announced her divorce and Blake Lively, best known as the star of the prime time teen soap *Gossip Girl* (the CW 2007–12), announced her pregnancy, on their respective lifestyle sites. Some of the sites, like Lively's Preserve, have had financial or publicity trouble and folded quickly. But all utilize motherhood as part of their self-brand identity and, essentially, as an avenue through which to transition their identity from "extraordinary" movie star to "ordinary" woman. New momism still mandates maternity for these women to justify and support this move, and motherhood works as a marker of their down-to-earth authenticity bridging the glamor of celebrity and the intimacy of Internet screens and recommendations for beauty products, food, self-care, and household goods. This chapter analyzes the conjunction of three distinct elements of twenty-first century life brought together by celebrity-helmed lifestyle blogs and consumer goods companies: mommy culture and mommy blogging; new modes of celebrity that emphasize authenticity and access over larger-than-life glamor; and the capitalization of the self-brand.

Reese Witherspoon, Oscar-winning actress, successful movie producer, and newly minted lifestyle brand founder, posted the following caption on a March 2015 Instagram photo:

> Starting today, the organization @LeanInOrg, which encourages women to #leanin and reach their goals at work and at home, is asking us to celebrate the men in our lives who love, help, and support us daily! Husband, dad, brother, grandpa—do you have an example of a man who you are thankful for? Share a photo tagged with the hashtag #LeanInTogether. I want to see!.... (And don't they deserve it?!)[1]

The photo accompanying this caption is an adorable snapshot of father and son, Witherspoon's husband holding hands and gazing lovingly at their young son, both decked out in wellies and rain gear in front of (presumably) the family home. In the caption, Witherspoon plays both adoring mother and wife, and Lean In feminist. The rest of Witherspoon's social media feed is a mixture of family life, Hollywood friends and red carpet events, books by women Witherspoon is reading and optioning for her film production company, and promotional shots for her lifestyle company Draper James. It forms a fairly complex tapestry of female friendship, professional collectivity or support among women, mothering charming children, and catalog images of Witherspoon wearing or using Draper James clothing and accessories. The feed collects and gives equal weight to images and messages that claim overt feminism and pictures of consumption, self-expression through beauty products and fashion, and the gushing of contemporary motherhood that seem distinctly postfeminist. This postfeminist outlook is emphasized by the hashtag in this particular post, sponsored by Lean In, Facebook COO Sheryl Sandberg's social media based feminist community building organization, which encourages women to "lean in" and more aggressively promote their own interests at work and at home. While trying to make its feminism more inclusive and welcoming to men, Lean In has been criticized for its exclusivity in targeting highly educated, well-off, corporate career women. Like the UN Women He For She campaign, helmed by another Hollywood actress, Emma Watson, #LeanInTogether requires women to make themselves and their feminism non-threatening for men. That softening of a feminist message smacks of the choice feminism Angela McRobbie describes in which women with a certain amount of social or financial power seem to choose to exploit themselves for their own gain.[2] Witherspoon's caption encourages giving men explicit credit for precisely the care work feminists have long fought to have recognized as work when women do it. Thus, Witherspoon's self-brand, as collated in her social media presence, reveals the juncture of often frustrating but still clearly thriving postfeminism with emerging celebrity or elite feminisms that are careful to distance themselves from stridency or direct political activism. It is through representations of stars' motherhood that this clash is often negotiated.

Pushing back against the policy and rhetoric of the "War on Women" during and after the Great Recession, new feminisms began to emerge alongside the "new domesticity" that framed many women's involuntary retreat from the workforce as a return to old-fashioned, make-it-yourself values and micro-entrepreneurialism. Lean In is one of these emergent feminisms, and Witherspoon's activism on their behalf, in the feminized space of social media, inside the frame of maternalism, emphasizes its contradictory and negotiated relationship to postfeminist domesticity, mommy culture, and hyper-femininity. This chapter examines celebrity women's lifestyle companies and the ways in which women, like Witherspoon and actresses Gwyneth Paltrow, Jessica Alba, and Monica Potter, navigate the porous boundaries between postfeminism and emergent new feminisms, and in so doing, highlight the classed and raced performances of motherhood necessary to access this mode of female "success" and entrepreneurship. Motherhood, children, and family are the key terrains on which these female celebrity lifestyle entrepreneurs make the shift from "extraordinary" actor to "ordinary" self-brand.

So far, this book has focused on wealthy women performing motherhood and creating unified self-brands to promote luxury consumer products outside of or after their work on "quality reality" programs. This chapter moves the scene of analysis to a parallel "quality" venue—online celebrity lifestyle brands and retail outlets. I extend the theoretical notion of quality from TV to the Internet because the polished audiovisual interface of high-end online lifestyling pursues the same quality consumer, with the same agenda of affective bonding morphing into purchasing as we have seen in the "quality reality" television discussed in earlier chapters. In the same way that reality television does, these lifestyle websites require celebrities to perform authenticity and their "real" selves in order to win and maintain fans invested enough to cross platforms from cinema or TV screens to social media and online shopping. The primary distinction is that while reality performers are famous for being themselves, these lifestyle entrepreneurs were famous first for film and television acting. As a result, their lifestyle brands represent a shift for them from public performances of glamor, film promotion, and even occasional requests for privacy to a performance of a more intimate "real" self. They do this via the obviously professional yet still seemingly personal writing, curating, and promoting of products as well as via the sharing of domestic scenes, holiday snaps, and personal stories of their family life on a mixture of social media and their own online brand outlets. The celebrity blogs and lifestyle companies discussed in this chapter frame motherhood not as an obstacle to career or fulfillment but as the impetus for retreating (albeit incompletely) from Hollywood in favor of feminized, domesticated entrepreneurialism that often masks business acumen and intense labor with the love of children, home and well-being. In creating marketable fantasies for their consumers, these women and their companies demonstrate recent changes in celebrity that emphasize intimacy and authenticity, and as aspirational spaces, they offer insight into the modes of motherhood, entrepreneurialism, and feminism that are culturally valued and idealized.

Quality has long been a discourse through which television scholars have legitimated the discipline and marked out which texts are worthy of study.[3] Markers of quality shift over time but at the core of quality discussions are higher production values, more affluent target audiences, and a critical respect that elevates a bad object like television—or online shopping—to an acceptable and even culturally valued definer of middle-class tastes. Inevitably, this perspective canonizes certain styles and genres and denigrates others, often perpetuating assumptions about gendered, raced, and classed representations, target audiences, and taste cultures. Feminist scholars, in particular, have pushed back against this hierarchizing tendency, arguing, as observed in previous chapters, that labeling certain genres, networks, and styles of television *not* quality hides or ignores the cultural functions of those programs and discounts entire genres like reality.[4] Extending the quality moniker to reality TV, as Jane Feuer has, is not intended to create similar hierarchies and blind spots within this supposedly low genre, but instead is intended to highlight the ways in which concerns about quality aesthetics, quality demographics, and quality brands are already at work in these spaces. Michael Z. Newman and Elana Levine have critiqued the too-often masculinizing effects of "legitimating" discourses like quality, so perhaps the biggest innovation of using the word quality within discussions of reality TV is to use this masculinized discourse within such a feminized space, offering "trash" TV similar weight to high-brow dramas and highlighting it, as Brenda Weber urges, for the analysis of its key cultural functions.

Extending these discourses of quality to another denigrated feminized space, online-first lifestyle brands, aims to accomplish the same goals in this adjacent venue. Television programs, and reality television in particular, cannot be understood as insular texts, but are always automatically part of a textual system that includes professional, corporate-sanctioned paratexts, various modes of viewer engagement, and online, print, and televised gossip and criticism. Vitally, for the arguments made here regarding the links between women being "real" moms on TV and in brand culture, that textual system includes the commoditized self-brand and the consumer products brands created, promoted and maintained by reality performers outside and alongside the purview of the television producers, distributors, and promoters. Indeed, Maureen Ryan has argued that lifestyle blogging and television are converging in some genres, citing Ree Drummond, for example, whose successful blog *The Pioneer Woman* (thepioneerwoman.com), along with branded novels and cookbooks, became a Food Network television show as well (*The Pioneer Woman*, 2011–Present).[5] So, in one sense, this chapter simply begins with the Internet platforms and commodities where previous chapters ended. If reality television performers have to create "transmediated continuity" to achieve career longevity and be fully self-branded, complete postfeminist subjects, websites like Witherspoon's Draper James accomplish the same goal for stars of scripted TV and cinema.[6] Within postfeminist and recessionary culture, even the glamor, prestige, and wealth of being Oscar winning actresses do not insulate the likes of Witherspoon and Paltrow from participating in retreatist narratives and domesticating their brand images within the frames of motherhood and family, in order to find entrepreneurial spaces to establish brand and career longevity in the face of Hollywood's consistent ageism and sexism.

As throughout this book, I choose to analyze "quality" brand outlets aimed at relatively elite consumers in order to understand what is most culturally valued, particularly in times of highly visible, entrenched inequality. To that end, this chapter focuses on the polished professional aesthetics, the aura of classy celebrity, and the representations of ordinariness in Witherspoon's Draper James and Gwyneth Paltrow's GOOP, and sets GOOP's luxurious excesses and relative distance from domestic scenes in contrast to the classed or racialized performances of authenticity inherent in the branding of Monica

Potter's Monica Potter Home, and Jessica Alba's The Honest Company. I argue that demanding professional labor is framed as a retreat inspired by motherhood and family, and I examine the ways in which these brands and their founders embody the tensions between postfeminist entrepreneurialism and emergent feminisms that reveal the unfortunate limitations of the latter.

Reese Witherspoon, Monica Potter, and Regional Retreatism

In theorizing the retreatist narrative common in postfeminist films of the 1990s and early 2000s, Diane Negra uses the Reese Witherspoon-starring romantic comedy *Sweet Home Alabama* (2002) as one of her illustrative examples of a hometown story in which a woman in her thirties leaves behind a high-powered career in the big city to find love, family, and happiness in the small town where she grew up.[7] Coincidentally, in her 30s, Witherspoon herself has shaped her career and persona to fit an only slightly updated version of this narrative arc. In 2015, she launched her lifestyle company Draper James—tag line Grace & Charm—first online and then with a flagship bricks and mortar store in her native Nashville, Tennessee. "Pretty Please," says Witherspoon, half smiling and looking coyly into the camera in an introductory video on draperjames.com, "It's not just a way to get what you want, it's a lifestyle."[8] The accompanying text explains Witherspoon's love for the elegant South in which she grew up and describes starting this new business venture as a return home. Unspoken but visible in her personal Instagram account and the gossip discourse around her and publicity for the site are that she returned to Nashville with her husband to raise their child, a toddler with the conveniently brand-appropriate name Tennessee. Like most lifestyle companies, Draper James focuses on fashion, accessories, and home décor but includes added shopping sections like Hostess Gifts and a line of stationery "for every occasion—and there are a lot of occasions" that emphasize the brand's claims to Southern charm and politeness. Witherspoon evokes her grandparents, the company's namesakes, and notions of family roots and community when she describes Draper James in publicity materials. Her grandmother, Dorothea Draper, "exuded elegance. She didn't have a lot of dresses, but no matter what she wore, she always made heads turn." Invoking her grandmother's style despite her thrift ("she didn't have a lot of dresses") and her grandfather James Witherspoon's adage that "good manners and great style go hand in hand"[9] creates a sense of authenticity by linking Witherspoon to a family history and a specific regional identity.[10] Furthermore, like the paparazzi photos of Rachel Zoe's children that made them mini-brand spokesmen for her fashion-centric business, so the images of Witherspoon's children, especially the youngest, Tennessee, provide a context for her new venture comfortably in keeping with contemporary postfeminist mommy culture. Via gossip and social media, Witherspoon's kids frame her retreatist narrative and help brand her just another (wealthy, white) Southern mom. Her social media presence features frequent pictures of her three kids and the occasional photo series #toddlerbreakfast with shots of waffles with faces made from fruit and bacon. These family snapshots and the story of Witherspoon as a working mother returning home are seamlessly integrated into the social media feed-cum-brand outlets that also promote Draper James products and events and emphasize white Southernness with quaint sayings and Nashville locations alongside pictures of Witherspoon's glamorous Hollywood friends and red carpet events. Her social media presence also includes more purposefully feminist promotions like the #LeanInTogether post or promotions of female authors or Witherspoon's upcoming films.

Witherspoon's social media feed, lifestyle brand, and indeed the contemporary iteration of her entire star text serve multiple cultural functions, with motherhood and Southernness authenticating postfeminist norms of consumption and feminine prettiness, while her screen presence and, in particular, her behind-the-scenes production work push high-profile paid female labor and more complex performances of femininity into the limelight. This dual address, combining a lifestyle of family, elegance, and polite manners with strident support of female writers and complex female characters, offers a window into the complexities, frustrations, and limitations of living within this cultural moment when feminism may be reemerging in some forms but has by no means definitively superseded postfeminism.

In fact, the skill with which Witherspoon lives in both the feminist and postfeminist worlds is part of the reason her persona remains well-liked and does not fall victim to some of the scorn aimed at stars perceived to be elitist, unrelatable, or inauthentic, like Gwyneth Paltrow.[11] This may be due, in part, to the careful separation she maintains between her lifestyle brand and her film production business. In contrast to the postfeminist emphasis on home and family evident in Draper James, in 2012 Witherspoon co-founded the production company Pacific Standard with her business partner, veteran producer Bruna Papandrea. The company's mission is to foster female voices and, thus far, the focus has been on optioning books by women authors and ushering them through to film or television production.[12] Witherspoon stars or plans to star in many (*Wild* [2014], *Hot Pursuit* [2015], *Big Little Lies* [HBO, 2016–]), but not all (*Gone Girl* [2014]) of the productions on her company's slate, but all have substantial, complex parts for women. This has the nice byproduct of boosting those female authors' book sales, but it also demonstrates female entrepreneurialism with the direct, stated, feminist intent of fostering female creativity and addressing Hollywood's representational gender gap. Witherspoon is explicit about her company's goal to support female writers, and *Wild* and *Gone Girl*, while perhaps not intersectional or radical feminist texts, centralize well-developed female characters whose goals are self-focused rather than romantic or maternal. Witherspoon's Southern-inflected, retreatist lifestyle company and the rest of her self-brand exemplify a culture in transition from neoliberal entrepreneurial postfeminism to something still emerging.

Monica Potter offers another illustration of regionalized retreat, this time invoking nostalgia for white working class Midwesternness. Mrs. Potter is the original name of the lifestyle and household products brand created by actress Monica Potter, best known for her role as Kristina Braverman in the ensemble family drama *Parenthood* (NBC 2010–15). Now known as Monica Potter Home, the Mrs. in the brand's initial name enshrines marriage and family as the central markers of identity, and much more than other celebrity brands, Potter's brand and marketing materials feature her own home. Her daughter Molly, who was 11 years old at the time of writing, is also an active participant in marketing efforts on the brand's website and social media. Like Witherspoon's Southern-inflected brand, Potter emphasizes a specific regional identity and nostalgic discourses of returning to childhood homes. In 2015, Potter opened a flagship bricks and mortar store in suburban Cleveland, Ohio, and completing her retreatist narrative, she re-purchased her childhood home and is refurbishing it along with her sisters in order to have a home and business base near the store. In addition to the physical retail space, Mrs. Potter situates most of its production in and around Cleveland. "Each product," the website claims, repeating its version of Witherspoon's avowal that as much as possible of her company's production takes place in the American South, and Jessica Alba's insistence on the natural and earth-friendly origins of her products, "is developed naturally and made by the hardworking people of the Ohio Valley."[13] In the same way Draper James's tagline "Grace & Charm" emphasizes Southernness, Potter's brand emphasizes the historically working class manufacturing culture of the Midwest. The brand consistently uses the word artisans rather than product developers or fabricators to emphasize the contemporary value placed on authenticity, DIY, and smallness emblematic of the recession era "new domesticity." Potter speaks frequently about a lifelong desire to create jobs in her home region, implicitly invoking earlier, pre-Great Recession economic devastation created by major corporations closing factories and relocating out of the "Rust Belt" in favor of cheap overseas labor.[14] Thus, the rhetoric of one recession, of retreatism, domesticity, and individual entrepreneurialism, is mobilized to salve the region-specific wounds of a previous economic disaster. Furthermore, the domesticity of that earlier, pre-feminist era shores up the "appropriate" femininity of Potter's home products brand.

Alongside the authenticity evoked by the regional specificity of the working class Midwestern city is an emphasis on natural products and an unspoken but pervasive whiteness. This whiteness is aesthetic, as in widespread use of blank white space in the logo design, site layout, and imagery on the brand's webpage. It is also racialized in the near total absence of people of color from the site alongside the emphasis on highly skilled artisans rather than the much more racially diverse workers affected by earlier recessions or, indeed, who make up more than 50 percent of Cleveland's population.[15] The rhetoric of the natural is never framed as a gesture toward sustainability or environmental concerns but instead is another form of retreat.

DIY beauty and cleaning products are relatively cost effective but time consuming, perfect for a nostalgia-inflected return to the domestic sphere. Following tips and recipes in the website's DIY section builds an affection for and commitment to the brand that, ideally for Potter and her business associates, will spill over into the Shop or Retail Store tabs of the homepage. In other words, the investment of fan labor, done in their own homes, transitions into identifying with the brand and purchasing its products.

Potter also borrows authenticity from her most well-known and most recent fictional television role. Unlike the larger-than-life movie stardom of Witherspoon, Alba, or Paltrow, Potter's star text is most tightly linked to the smaller scale, more intimate understanding of television stardom. Potter's specific role as a mother, wife, and activist/entrepreneur on a domestic family drama actually creates a stockpile of authenticity from which she can draw when transitioning from performer to lifestyle brand creator. A core part of Potter's *Parenthood* character are her heroic motherhood and intensely visible affective labor parenting a child with Asperger's Syndrome, battling cancer, and running for mayor, to name just a few of the ways in which her character surmounts obstacles and achieves goals through emotional connections with friends, family, and community. The show's realist aesthetic and improvisational acting strengthen the link between character and performer, creating a self-brand almost like a reality performer. Potter herself then strengthens that link posting behind the scenes photos of herself with other cast members, all of whom appear to be close friends, further blurring the boundary between fictional family and real life "workplace family." Thus, Potter brings with her an already well-established sheen of authenticity, and the values—family, affect, work ethic, and public service—she foregrounds in her lifestyle company's identity are the same ones foregrounded in her character's identity. In a video from the Monica Potter Home site, for example, Potter discusses her "inventor" dad and "homemaker" mom and describes her upbringing in a "blue-collar family, a hard-working family."[16] In the video, she visits some of her "makers," the people who create and manufacture the products she sells, and everyone hugs and smiles—Potter even cries when she sees one of the products because she's so excited. The video functions to create a small business "family," performing affection and sentimentality with lyrical music, soft focus, over-exposure, and the laughing, crying, and emotional responses of the workplace family in the video.

The video serves as an integral part of the blog's aesthetic. For any lifestyle blog, its aesthetic and navigability are the first units of meaning that a user encounters with the brand. The site's structure, color palette, and layout are carriers of cultural meaning just as the products, stars, and promotional texts are. For Potter, there is an investment in whiteness in the brand's web design that evokes cleanliness and calm. Richard Dyer traces "the slippage between white as hue, skin and symbol" at least as far back as Shakespeare and continuing in visual art and literature through to the present. He further notes the "explicit symbolic sense of moral and also aesthetic superiority" associated with the color white.[17] Alongside the relative lack of people of color visible on the site, the aesthetic whiteness gives consumers an idea of who the intended audience is, of who this lifestyle is for. Monica Potter Home is not alone in this sense; Paltrow's GOOP also makes ample use of white space. Witherspoon's Draper James offers a slightly wider color palette in its site design and fabrics, but its regional identity is deeply invested in a whiteness underscored by the unacknowledged racial history of black slavery. And as I have noted throughout this book, motherhood and domesticity may be the most valued forms of femininity in the early twenty-first century but that most valued and celebrated way of being a woman often reinforces an implicit over-valuing of whiteness. The working class Midwestern bootstrapping, job-creating ethos Potter's brand relies on is also a specifically white working class.

Figure 3.1 A still image from the YouTube promotional video "I-X Christmas Connection Blooper Reel" shows Potter in her all white and off-white home workshop. YouTube https://www.youtube.com/watch?v=nk9w-xv8HK4.

The photo above, taken from a site video called "I-X Christmas Connection Blooper Reel" demonstrates the pervasively white aesthetic of Potter's home, website, and even the products themselves.[18] As in this image, Potter often wears little makeup with her hair tied back messily and held in place or covered with bandanas. The sunlight from a prominent window in the background overexposes and washes out the image. Her platinum hair, white and beige wardrobe and décor emphasize the setting's bright sunshine and white paint, while the occasional blue bandana semiotically recalls her blue-collar and working-class Midwestern roots. Furthermore, even the existence of a blooper reel emphasizes Potter's persona or brand identity as a "real" mom.

Jessica Alba, Gwyneth Paltrow, and Performances of Authenticity

Just as children and family help frame the retreatist narratives that support the Draper James and Monica Potter Home brands, motherhood is frequently a way for a star to cultivate a market-friendly air of authenticity that is also suited to the labor-intensive style of maternity mandated by contemporary mommy culture. Moreover, motherhood then becomes a way to mask entrepreneurial labor as affective maternal labor, mimicking the efforts on the part of some feminist groups to soften their feminism by appealing to men. Film and television actress Jessica Alba (perhaps most widely known for her role as Sue Storm in the *Fantastic Four* [2005, 2007] films), for example, tells the origin story of her own lifestyle venture, The Honest Company, saying:

> 'When I became a mom, I finally became the person I am, that I always should have been,' she says. 'It's the most satisfying job in the world. But, it can also be overwhelming and confusing. I created The Honest Company to help moms and to give all children a better, safer start.'[19]

This description of becoming her full adult self only upon bearing children echoes the sentiments represented in the pregnancy storylines discussed in Chapter One. Alba makes herself relatable by talking about how "overwhelming and confusing" new motherhood can be, but she also credits motherhood as the impetus for her business, framing maternity as the economic pathway to public life via entrepreneurialism, not a career obstacle as it is so often in the US where parental leave is minimal and childcare is expensive. As with Witherspoon, the private realm of motherhood and family become tools with which to maintain audience engagement and "relatability," simultaneously creating social meaning: Motherhood is somehow essential to both an aspirational domestic-centered lifestyle *and* female, even feminist, entrepreneurialism; motherhood is the key to full subjectivity in private and public life.

To move back and forth from TV or movie star to lifestyle brand, these actresses must tweak the relationship between their public selves and paid performances, and performances of their private selves. Because the lifestyle entrepreneurs in this chapter are all already celebrities, their pre-existing stardom is a primary tool with which they build their self-brands. Stars have always been understood as an amalgam of ordinary and extraordinary, aspiration and mundanity.[20] As celebrity culture has expanded far beyond actors, intimacy and immediacy have become requirements even for A-list stars, particularly for women. The "transmediated continuity" that elevates degraded forms of notoriety like reality performance to longer-term celebrity and financial security increasingly applies to more traditional modes of celebrity—film and television stars—as well as the reality performers for whom the term was coined.[21] The companies and modes of promotion used by Witherspoon, Potter, Paltrow, Alba and other celebrity lifestyle entrepreneurs operate in this mode, similarly requiring performances of a behind-the-scenes "real" self, to build the affective bonds with fans that turn viewers into shoppers. Before the era of pervasive social media, theorists debated distinctions between cinema and television stardom. James Bennett argued that because of the domesticity, quotidian intimacy, and small scale of television screens, TV actors could be "personalities," but never the extraordinary present/absent "stars" of cinema.[22] In a technological and cultural milieu that overvalues proximity, touch, and appearances of intimacy, however, the casual dailiness of interaction has become a desirable way for stars to spread their brand across platforms and help prolong their careers. The Internet, where social media communications and lifestyle browsing and shopping take place, is often more intimate even than television's traditional position in the living room. For the affluent audiences hailed by the "quality" programs and products discussed throughout this book, the Internet, in the form of a mobile phone, is typically carried everywhere one goes, often in the tight confines of a trouser pocket, and used at home, at work, in transit, and even in bed. And "[t]hough individuals may still emerge into the public eye through some sort of talent or public performance, it is the audience's engagement with their private selves that increasingly defines celebrity status and attendant social meanings of the celebrity image."[23] Unwittingly writing about a soon-to-be lifestyle entrepreneur Lauren Conrad, Elizabeth Affuso argues that the push to deemphasize performers' fame work in reality docusoaps like MTV's *The Hills* (2006–10) reflects the shift in celebrity culture to emphasize the mundane over the extraordinary.[24] The same process is at work when celebrities must deemphasize the branding work of creating and revealing more of their "real" selves to build a lifestyle brand.

It is a delicate balancing act, of course, for celebrities to perform this behind-the-scenes authenticity well enough to maintain fans while remaining extraordinary enough to be aspirational figures who inspire imitation and consumption. Gwyneth Paltrow was a pioneer in the lifestyle market when she launched GOOP in 2008. Perhaps in part because the luxury outlet, "where food, shopping, and mindfulness collide" launched around the same time financial markets began collapsing and global recession impacted all but the wealthiest, Paltrow's brand and by extension Paltrow herself, have been the subject of fairly harsh critiques for elitism since its unveiling.[25] Some of the most intense backlash has come at moments when Paltrow has disclosed personal information about her family or her daily life, divulging its complete lack of ordinariness. In the spring of 2014, for example, Paltrow separated from her husband of ten years and announced it on GOOP, under the headline "Conscious Uncoupling." The phrase, which Paltrow later revealed was not hers but was chosen by the site's editorial director, was immediately, soundly, mocked.[26] One commentator called the phrase "utterly obnoxious" but also noted (albeit with a tongue-in-cheek tone) that transforming the painful personal event of divorce into an opportunity to educate the public in vaguely spiritual mindfulness, marked her as truly a star, inhabiting a world so removed from the every day that even her divorce was special.[27] Around the same time, Paltrow gave an interview about being a newly single working mother in which she said,

> I think it's different when you have an office job, because it's routine and, you know, you can do all the stuff in the morning and then you come home in the evening. When you're shooting a movie, they're like, 'We need you to go to Wisconsin for two weeks,' and then you work 14 hours a day and that part of it is very difficult. I think to have a regular job and be a mom is not as, of course there are challenges, but it's not like being on set.[28]

Again, the backlash was swift and pervasive against what was perceived as an overt and egregiously tone-deaf statement of privilege.[29] What was not widely reported was that Paltrow was not comparing her life on movie sets to women struggling to get by without all of her fortune and available support systems, but rather comparing her relatively regular hours work at GOOP to shooting films. Of course Paltrow's statement is immensely privileged; however, what the backlash reveals is the erasure of the labor of brand management, blogging, and lifestyle work, as well as the ways in which a star's relationship to motherhood and work can often define her public perception. Unlike Alba, who portrays her work as springing from and in service to motherhood, Paltrow's brand is more about self-care and luxury, setting her up as a perfect villain within a culture obsessed with labor-intensive, self-defining, and—essentially—self-sacrificing motherhood. Paltrow's brand persists and is objectively a successful business, but the consistency with which she and GOOP are villainized, I argue, is because she does not publicly perform motherhood very often and because she does not claim a retreatist identity. Instead, she presents a lavish, jet-setting, exotic, "mindful" brand identity that seems utterly distant from both the lived experiences of most middle-class consumers and from the contemporary image of successful female entrepreneurialism, which "should" always be framed through the domestic and the maternal.

While Paltrow and her business are not likely to suffer financially as a consequence of this devaluing of certain kinds of work, it represents a common experience of non-celebrity mommy and lifestyle bloggers whose labor is hidden or framed as passion and, therefore, does not require effort or remuneration. Arguably, the online self-revelatory or image-crafting work necessary to build a celebrity lifestyle brand took inspiration from the more common practices of mommy blogging and social media sharing, perhaps contributing to the myth of feasibly earning substantial income from the domestic and care work of motherhood. Emily Matchar argues for the feminist potential of personal mommy blogs, or at least the hope on the part of writers that blogging is an act of community, even of "revolution." She writes, "Feminists have long said that women should be paid for domestic work. Now, at least sometimes, they can be."[30] Similarly, Maureen Ryan argues for "the domestic context as a site of rich narrative and identity work" in much the same way that within mommy culture, motherhood itself is represented as identity work.[31] Of course, women bloggers are not being paid for their domestic work, but for *writing* about their domestic work. They are being paid not for their housework or childcare, which they would do anyway, but for narrativizing, aestheticizing, and rendering their housework appealing, work that includes creating and maintaining the self- as-brand, and the affective labor of building and maintaining a fan base— in short, fame work. The most successful mommy bloggers, those who are able to support themselves and their families financially from the advertising money earned from their blogging also must manage their businesses or hire and manage employees (often family members for this subset of bloggers) to keep track of finances, promotions, and advertising sales. Far from being paid for doing housework, these women have created small businesses that they own and run *in addition* to their housework. Running a small business from home, making one's family the locus of all affective and paid labor, is the fulfillment of contemporary neoliberal rhetoric and reframes a retreat to DIY and homemade often thrust upon women by economic hardship and recession as a noble and profitable choice. The illusion that they are getting paid for housework makes it possible to represent this work as revolutionary and feminist, when in fact it fits comfortably into postfeminist frameworks of choice that hide women's writing and business skills by focusing so intensely on seemingly joyful, chosen, domestic spaces discussed and celebrated on their blogs. In some ways, it is Gwyneth Paltrow's unwillingness to fully integrate her work and life spaces in this postfeminist mode that sets her apart from (and apparently above) women's daily negotiations between roles of wife, mother, and paid worker or entrepreneur. That is not to argue that Paltrow is a feminist. In fact, in contrast to Witherspoon and Jessica Alba, she does not claim that title within or outside the bounds of her GOOP brand.

Nonetheless, some have argued that for non-celebrity mothers who blog, the public act of writing offers valuable community and visibility for women who might feel stuck at home, and gives them the potential for economic gain from domestic and affective labor. Celebrities, though, combine this practice with lucrative commerce, something most bloggers are unable to achieve without the famous person's pre-existing capital—in the form of money, support teams of publicists, business managers and assistants, and fame itself. Because of the time, money, and labor required to make a domestic or lifestyle blog profitable, an extremely small number of amateurs or "micro-celebrities" can achieve that goal.[32] Yet, Lori Kido Lopez calls mommy blogging, a potentially "radical act," describing how women find validation for their often invisible experiences and labor via the act of reading, writing, and commenting on blogs.[33] This potential is enhanced by blogging's "network" rather than "broadcast" structures of communication, emphasizing the feedback loop, rather than the top-down structures of blogging circles.[34] Lopez makes a utopian argument that "Women who blog about their children are transforming their personal narratives of struggle and challenge into interactive conversations with other mothers, and in so doing, are beginning to expand our notion of motherhood, women bloggers and the mother's place within the public sphere."[35] Julie Wilson and Emily Chivers Yochim have made similar arguments about social pinning, that is, saving images, articles, tips, and other tidbits onto public pinboards on Pinterest and other social media, where others can follow, comment, like, or re-pin/re-post them. In a practice they call "pinning happiness," Wilson and Yochim argue that pinning "happy scenes, good habits, and best practices, fun activities, and thoughtful ruminations on the meaning of life" offers a reminder of the "potential and promise of family happiness."[36] In essence, each pinboard curates an aspirational lifestyle in the same way lifestyle brands do, except as a leisure practice rather than a directly consumer-oriented one. I argue that happiness pins offer alternate affective potentials as well—hate reading, as just one example, is the practice of reading or following a social media account that provokes rage in order to experience the catharsis of those negative feelings or even to cultivate a sense of superiority or resistance to dominant cultural narratives. Tiffany Beveridge's satirical pinboard Quinoa My Imaginary Well-Dressed Toddler Daughter is perhaps the most recognizable example of often playful alternate ways of engaging with this element of mommy culture. The captions she adds to children's fashion photos, naming the models things like Quinoa, Chevron, and Hashtag and describing their ennui, playfully but ruthlessly skewer the wealthy, overinvested parents of mommy culture. Nonetheless, the inherent aspirationalism of these social media practices, like the community building of blogging, constitutes what Lauren Berlant calls an "intimate public." Aimée Morrison argues that,

> practices common to personal mommy blogging replicate some of the difficulties that Berlant finds plague women's culture, undermining this public's capacity to act in the broader public sphere: that is, to effect social change. In particular, in common with women's culture more broadly, personal mommy blogging blunts the political force of its critique of the nature and experience of womanhood in contemporary society by maintaining a rigid separation of its intimate public from mainstream public culture.[37]

In one sense, celebrity mommy blogging-cum-lifestyling expands this intimate public into a more mainstream public sphere. Indeed, each of these celebrity-owned lifestyle companies includes a charity or service component, framing their private enterprise ventures as directly in service of social change and the public good. Yet, to return to Witherspoon's example, often any actively political statements or overtly feminist actions are compartmentalized away from the lifestyle brand itself. In Witherspoon's case, her film production company's direct statement of female collectivity is separate from the emphasis on domestic etiquette and traditional femininity in the Draper James brand. For all the lifestyle brands discussed here, the charitable initiatives are found only at the very bottom of the sites with small, de-emphasized links alongside links to contact information and return policies. These philanthropic ventures are another way to transition from acting (work in which labor is purposely and carefully hidden behind an attempt at "authentic" or realist performance) to consumer products sales, the performance of a disinterest in capitalist gain giving these businesses the feminized frame of philanthropic ventures. As Alison Trope argues, "Historically, the ideals of and everyday work of philanthropy neatly have adhered to the prescribed domestic and nurturing roles historically assigned to white women."[38] Paltrow's framing of GOOP as a place to cultivate "mindfulness" serves this goal, as does the job creation and economic revitalization rhetoric centralized in Monica Potter Home's brand descriptions and Witherspoon's insistence on American, and when possible local Southern labor. For Jessica Alba, this philanthropic frame comes in the form of environmentalism, and the rhetoric of "natural" products. Additionally, Draper James, The Honest Company, and GOOP all focus their corporate charitable giving on educational and other youth-oriented charities. Only Witherspoon's company ventures so far as to focus on girls, citing Girls, Inc. "helping young women become entrepreneurs, effective leaders, and creators of social change" as their primary beneficiary.[39] In the same vein, the careful choice of organizations to receive donations and promotions deflects potential controversy and reemphasizes the women's maternal, caring role, extending it from their own families to all children. This focus keeps their political activity firmly within feminized bounds and functions more as another way for wealthy celebrities to manage their image and perform a rejection of commercial gain than as an activist statement. Discussing her Honest Company, Jessica Alba asserts that,

> the core values, passion and principles we share at Honest.com lay a strong foundation of good intentions to help 'change the world.' How will we turn our genuine intentions and strong beliefs that our children deserve better into a business and cultural revolution?[40]

As this book argues, mommy culture is an active, even formative part of contemporary neoliberalism that Alba's explicit linkage of a business revolution with a cultural revolution clearly restates. For Alba and all the celebrity lifestylers and non-celebrity bloggers discussed here, the family is a capitalist economic unit as well as the locus for social change. Unfortunately, then, this mode of commerce and this type of intimate public loses the radical potential of mommy blogging and too often reinforces distinctly marked class and race boundaries, mobilizing discourses of individualism, neoliberalism, and commercial solutions to social problems.

One such commercial solution is Alba's "natural," "eco-friendly" brand solution to the personal effects of environmental degradation. The Honest Company was launched as a subscription mail order service to have diapers, detergents, and other baby-related goods free from toxic and allergenic chemicals delivered straight to one's home. It has since expanded into beauty, skincare, and cleaning products available via mail and appearing (in limited selection) in high-end US grocery chains like Whole Foods, as well as expensive local California and Los Angeles grocery chains Gelson's and Bristol Farms. However, unlike the high-cost luxury of Gwyneth Paltrow's curated and endorsed collection of goods, Honest Company products are also sold in trend-conscious but low-cost department store Target and big box store Costco. In these locations, they might still be priced above competition, but they aim at middle- and lower-middle-class consumers, supporting the brand's seemingly attainable populism. Each of these retail outlets echoes the whiff of "commodity activism" evident in Honest's emphasis on "natural" and "eco" products in fashionable packaging.[41] Gelson's and Bristol Farms are high end but local. Target has been criticized for exploiting overseas labor but participates in highly publicized (and localized) educational charities that help redeem its corporate reputation. Costco often bears critique for the sheer excess of its bulk-buying business model, yet it has a reputation for employee loyalty based on paying living wages, offering benefits to all full- and part-time employees, and capping executive pay. This combination of retail outlets then works symbiotically with the product brand and means Honest Company products reach affluent consumers while remaining within the reach of aspirational consumers. Because the mother-entrepreneurs in this chapter are already celebrities, they must negotiate the entrepreneurial self in ways that reality performers do not have to. One part of this process is to maintain the extraordinariness and wealth that make them aspirational figures without visible labor. Similarly, the fact that Alba's business venture is framed as stemming directly from her motherhood stresses the family as a capitalist economic unit, but the emphasis on the environment marks it as the locus for social change as well. The feel good combination of fashion, family-centric products, and environmental consciousness all work to create a comfortably feminized version of female entrepreneurialism and solve a social and political problem with shopping.

Because she is its face and figurehead, for Alba's company to continue to thrive, she must exhibit authenticity just like Witherspoon and Potter. Natural, environmental, and maternal discourses all contribute to her presentation as a "real" mom. Whereas Witherspoon and Potter's authenticity comes from regionalism and whiteness, however, Jessica Alba's performance of authenticity is connected to her ethnically inflected stardom. As she has moved beyond acting, Alba has cultivated an image rooted in visual and oral rhetoric of nature and the environment, all-fulfilling motherhood and passionate labor. Alba claims The Honest Company "isn't about money," but about helping other mothers create safe, happy, and fashionable environments for their children by purchasing "natural" and well-designed cleaning and baby products. In the process of pursuing her passion for entrepreneurial motherhood, however, Alba has landed on the cover of *Forbes* magazine as the co-founder and face of a $1 billion business.[42] I argue that Alba's incredibly lucrative brand relies on the conjunction of its natural and environmentally friendly rhetoric with Alba's ethnically inflected and peculiarly embodied stardom to create a mother-focused brand that throws "off-white" motherhood into relief against the other brands and stars dominating the celebmom lifestyle market.

This very successful brand relies on Alba's physical presence—her face and body—as a built-in celebrity endorsement. The aesthetic presentation of her image on Honest.com and related materials like her book, *The Honest Life: Living Naturally and True to You*, join with the rhetoric of "natural" and "eco" products to create this version of authenticity. In her work on Latino/a stardom in the US, Mary Beltrán argues that nonwhite stars carry an additional or particularly salient level of cultural meaning "given that social and racial hierarchies are both reflected in and reinforced by a nation's system of stardom."[43] Beltrán describes how Mexican American Alba's "initial lack of ethnic self-labeling in her career and her light tan, not brown, skin and girlish image have contributed to the perception that she is ethnically ambiguous of the degree most preferred by Hollywood ... Alba has achieved what Diane Negra has referred to as an 'off-white' image."[44] In this context, Negra notes that ethnicity can be mobilized "as the sign of sincerity and/or authenticity," thus functioning in the same way as the discourses of motherhood and nature that pervade Alba's work at The Honest Company.[45]

The Honest Company's About Us page spells out its brand identity. The stylish combination of soft lighting, straight lines, and industrial references in a neon sign and metal display table, if not the splashes of bright color, might easily turn up in a GOOP pop-up shop. But the profiles and family portraits of the Honest Company's founders, Alba and her partner Christopher Gavigan, illustrate some of the ways in which the brand negotiates notions of authenticity via racialized identities and the class address of their assumed consumer. In Alba's family portrait, she and her husband stride playfully down the middle of a tree-lined street, swinging one daughter between them, with the other daughter perched on Alba's hip. The family all wear a combination of khaki and medium blue tones. The sunshine filtered through green trees, tan skin, dark hair, and color in the family's clothing all give Alba's family portrait a warm golden glow. They are just a regular family out for a stroll in the park, the image seems to say. The sense of "realness" and natural setting are echoed in the cover image of Alba's lifestyle guide and memoire, *The Honest Life*, for sale on Honest.com. The book jacket features the same sun-kissed color palette and natural setting as the family photo. In this picture, Alba wears cream colored and pale pink, loose, drapey clothing as she sits barefoot on the ground, head turned to gaze and smile at the camera. Even the casual way her clothing slips off her shoulder and exposes bare legs suggests a warmth and ease that evokes a connection to nature and an accompanying authenticity. Along with the "honest" and "naturally" in the book's title, the brand themes of ecology, nature, and casual but on-trend fashion shine through.

Contrast Alba's portraits to Honest co-founder Christopher Gavigan's family photo on Honest.com's About Us page. His family is photographed seated in a formal portrait grouping on what appears to be a home's front lawn. Like Alba's family, they all wear blue and khaki and are placed with at least some natural green, although this is cultivated, manicured grass, not the seemingly wild-grown park trees in Alba's photo. The image is purposely overexposed, however, and the cold de-saturated look contrasts starkly with the warm colors of Alba's picture. Furthermore, the sun in this shot, rather than imparting the warmth it does in Alba's images, blurs white skin, blonde hair, pastel clothing, and even white stucco walls of the house in the background into a whitewashed mélange that almost makes facial features hard to pick out. Recalling as well the whiteness of Monica Potter's brand aesthetic and the specific sunny, overexposed image from Monica Potter Home analyzed above, this image makes the "off-white" nature of Alba's self-brand even more evident. Beltrán argues that crossover Latina stardom, including Alba's, is particularly embodied, "a hegemonic process that keeps nonwhite stars in their place."[46] Rather than disciplining or limiting Alba's stardom, however, in this context, the embodiment, connection to the natural environment and unspoken, ambiguous ethnicity "serves as a code for authenticity" that serves the brand effectively.[47] The intensified visibility of racial and economic inequalities that Negra argues led to a desire to reinvest or reemphasize ethnicity are heavily present in the early twenty-first century context of new momism as well,[48] and in the self-branded, celeb-mom lifestyle marketplace, authenticity is at a premium.

Powerful on its own, this version of authenticity gains traction in contrast to Gwyneth Paltrow's perception as extraordinary, elitist, and inauthentic. During a promotional interview for *The Honest Life,* a precursor to The Honest Company, Alba remarked that "Gwyneth Paltrow probably lives a very similar lifestyle, but I didn't grow up with a bunch of money, so my tips are much more grounded: repurposing things and making things at home."[49] Feeding into Paltrow's image as excessively wealthy and completely out of touch with middle class tastes, budgets, and schedules, Alba's comment, calculated to separate her from a perceived market competitor, sparked a discourse of celebrity feuding that persisted as each actress launched more products and as Paltrow continued to make public statements that were easy to frame as snobbish and exclusive. Furthermore, Paltrow's site GOOP enshrines an unspoken but privileged whiteness that, alongside Draper James and Monica Potter Home, throw the colorfulness of Honest.com and Alba's own "off-white" identity into relief. The GOOP site itself has a minimalist design with black type on a white background. Images on the front page heavily emphasize black and white with occasional dots of color. The brand identity page is also starkly different from Honest's. GOOP's "Meet the Team" page features crisp, cool black and white photography with Paltrow and her business partner CEO Lisa Gersh pictured individually (i.e. without families), cropped to medium close-ups with no context, and in the casual but distinctly professional look of loose-fitting white blouses and blazers. Both women are white with long blonde hair that, in the monochrome pictures, appears shades of white. Far from the warmth and informal approachability of Alba's images, Paltrow's are chic, minimalist, and cold. That contrast was exploited when gossip press created an alleged feud between the two lifestyle moguls based on Alba's critical comments.

Alice Marwick and danah boyd point out that celebrity feuds are performative, and just as much a part of image creation as more obviously crafted personal revelations.[50] Feuds also perpetuate the notion that women are always in competition with each other, stunting the likelihood of collective action, and emphasizing the juxtapolitical rather than political nature of women's intimate publics of mommy bloggers, or even lifestyle consumers. Via feud rhetoric, only one version of celebrity motherhood and lifestyling can emerge as the current "correct" way to navigate postfeminist celebrity, motherhood, and entrepreneurialism. More insidiously even than propagating the idea of female competition, the cultivation of a feud narrative between Paltrow and Alba perpetuates the idea that there is only cultural space "on top" for one woman at a time. Placing the burden of excessive wealth and privilege on Paltrow's website and persona thus scapegoats the discussion of actual contemporary inequalities into a celebrity feud. Much like the simultaneous aspiration to and denigration of the Bravo women discussed in Chapter Two, Paltrow in particular demonstrates the narrow boundaries within which female, self-branded entrepreneurs are permitted to function. Yet taken together, all of these celebrity lifestyle blogs reveal the complex negotiations among postfeminist, emerging feminist, and capitalist mandates necessary to be understood as successful female celebrities and entrepreneurs. In these negotiations, motherhood and the dexterity with which women are willing and able to present their motherhood as part of their self-brand and a framing device for their entrepreneurialism often sets the boundaries, not of their financial success, but of the perceived success of their representation within postfeminist, mother-centered popular culture.

Notes

1. Reese Witherspoon, Instagram, March 2015. Available online at https://www.instagram.com/p/z26J43ihY4/ (accessed December 14, 2015).
2. Angela McRobbie, "Postfeminism and Popular Culture," *Feminist Media Studies* 4.3 (2004): 254–64.
3. See for example, Charlotte Brunsdon, "Problems with Quality," *Screen* 31, no. 1 (1990): 67–90; Jane Feuer, Paul Kerr, and Tise Vahimagi, eds., *MTM: Quality Television* (London: BFI, 1984); Mark Jancovich and James Lyons,

Quality Popular Television: Cult TV, the Industry, and Fans (London: BFI, 2003). For a critique of quality TV discourse, see Michael Z. Newman and Elana Levine, *Legitimating Television* (New York: Routeldge, 2011).

4. Brenda Weber, "Trash Talk: The Gender Politics of Reality Television," *Reality Gendervisions: Sexuality and Gender on Transatlantic Reality TV* (Durham, NC: Duke University Press, 2014); Jane Feuer, "'Quality' Reality and the Bravo Media Reality Series," *Camera Obscura* 30.1 (2015): 185–95.

5. Maureen Ryan, "Feminist Housewife Blogger," Paper presented at the Society for Cinema and Media Studies Conference, Boston, MA (March 21–25, 2012).

6. Jennifer Lynn Jones and Brenda R. Weber, "Reality Moms, Real Monsters: Transmediated Continuity, Reality Celebrity, and the Female Grotesque," *Camera Obscura* 30.1 (2015): 11–39.

7. Diane Negra, *What a Girl Wants? Fantasizing the Reclamation of Self in Post-feminism* (London and New York: Routledge, 2009), 15–46.

8. "Who is Draper James?" Draper James. Available online at www.draperjames.com/about-us/ (accessed December 14, 2015).

9. Ibid.

10. Witherspoon's South is different than the South of *The Real Housewives of Atlanta* discussed in Chapter Two. Draper James paints a pretty picture of white Southernness that erases race from that regional identity. Yet of course the grace and charm of white Southernness relies on the history of black enslavement.

11. Witherspoon's image took a brief hit in April 2013 when her husband was pulled over and arrested for DUI. The actress was heard challenging police and asking if they knew who she was. She was arrested for disorderly conduct. Witherspoon apologized swiftly and publicly and never shied away from answering questions about the incident, citing panic at seeing her husband arrested to explain her actions. The openness and swiftness of her apology allowed the scandal to blow over quickly and without long-term damage to her image. See, for example, Stephanie Marcus, "Reese Witherspoon Opens Up about Her 2013 Disorderly Conduct Arrest," *Huffington Post* October 13, 2014. Available online at www.huffingtonpost.com/2014/10/13/reese-witherspoon-arrest_n_5978484.html (accessed February 8, 2016).

12. Rebecca Ford, "Reese Witherspoon on Her Production Company: 'We Support New Female Voices in Film,'" *Hollywood Reporter,* October 26, 2015. Available online at www.hollywoodreporter.com/news/reese-witherspoon-her-production-company-833137 (accessed April 10, 2016).

13. "Meet Monica Potter," *Monica Potter Home.* Available online at www.monicapotterhome.com/about-monica-potter/ (accessed February 9, 2016).

14. *Forbes* magazine listed Cleveland as one of their top 100 cities for business and careers in 2015. "The Best Places for Business and Careers," *Forbes* undated. Available online at www.forbes.com/best-places-for-business/ (accessed December 19, 2015).

15. "State and County Quick Facts," US Census Bureau 2010. Available online at http://quickfacts.census.gov/qfd/states/39/3916000.html (accessed February 18, 2016).

16. "A Sense of Comfort," Monica Potter Home, Video. Available online at www.monicapotterhome.com/monica-potter-home-sense-comfort/ (accessed December 19, 2015).

17. Richard Dyer, *White* (London: Routledge, 1997), 64, 70.

18. "I-X Christmas Blooper Reel," Monica Potter Home, Video. Available online at www.monicapotterhome.com/x-christmas-connection-blooper-reel/ (accessed December 19, 2015).
19. Jessica Alba, "Our Story: Who We Are," Honest.com. Available online at www. honest.com/about-us/who-we-are (accessed December 9, 2014).
20. Richard Dyer, *Stars* (London: BFI Press, 1979).
21. Jennifer Lynn Jones and Brenda R. Weber, "Reality Moms, Real Monsters: Transmediated Continuity, Reality Celebrity, and the Female Grotesque," *Camera Obscura* 30.1 (2015): 11–39.
22. James Bennett, "The Television Personality System: Televisual Stardom Revisited after Film Theory," *Screen* 49.1 (Spring 2008): 32–50.
23. Erin Meyers, "Gossip Blogs and 'Baby Bumps': The New Visual Spectacle of Female Celebrity in Gossip Media," *The Handbook of Gender, Sex, & Media*, Karen Ross, ed. (Oxford: Wiley-Blackwell Press, 2012), 67.
24. Affuso wrote before the show ended and could not have known that *The Hills'* star, Lauren Conrad, would go on to launch her own lifestyle brand at LaurenConrad.com in 2011. Elizabeth, Affuso "'Don't Just Watch It—Live It:' Technology, Corporate Partnership, and *The Hills*," *Jump Cut* 51 (Spring 2009). Available online at ejumpcut.org.
25. "What's Goop?" undated. Available online at http://goop.com/whats-goop/ (accessed December 15, 2015).
26. The divorce announcement is no longer on goop.com, but Psychologists Habib Sadeghi and Sherry Sami explain the term on the site: "Conscious Uncoupling," *GOOP*, undated. Available online at http://goop.com/conscious-uncoupling-2/ (accessed July 7, 2015). See also Allison Takeda, "Gwyneth Paltrow: 'It Wasn't My Idea to Call My Divorce Announcement a 'Conscious Uncoupling,'" *Us Weekly* August 3, 2015. Available online at http://goo.gl/ppEsnD (accessed December 15, 2015).
27. Daniel D'Addario, "Gwyneth Paltrow's Utterly Obnoxious 'Conscious Uncoupling' Letter Proves She's the Last Great Star," *Salon*, March 26, 2014. Available online at http://goo.gl/KRgfqB (accessed December 15, 2015).
28. Lily Harrison, "Gwyneth Paltrow's Post-Split Plans: Actress Reveals She's Taking a Break from Acting to Focus on Her Kids," March 26, 2014. Available online at Uk.eonline.com (accessed December 8, 2014).
29. The quote briefly became a hot topic of red carpet conversations, forcing other celebrity mothers to critique Paltrow, no matter how they attempted to evade the question or gently couch their answers. See, for example, Bruna Nessif, "Connie Britton Weighs In on Gwyneth Paltrow's Working Moms Comment, Talks Perks of Being a Single Parent," E! online, September 3, 2014. (accessed December 8, 2014); Stephanie Webber, "Busy Philips Reacts to Gwyneth Paltrow's Working Moms Comments, Says Being an Actress Is 'Not That Hard,'" *Us Weekly*, May 30, 2014. Available online (accessed December 8, 2014).
30. Emily Matchar, *Homeward Bound: Why Women Are Embracing the New Domesticity* (New York: Simon & Schuster, 2013), 59–60, Kindle Edition.
31. Maureen Ryan, "Feminist Housewife Blogger."
32. Alice Marwick and danah boyd, "To See and Be Seen: Celebrity Practice on Twitter," *Convergence* 17.2 (May 2011): 155.
33. Lori Kido Lopez, "The Radical Act of 'Mommy Blogging:' Redefining Motherhood Through the Blogosphere," *New Media & Society* 11.5 (2009): 729–47.

34. Aimée Morrison, "'Suffused by Feeling and Affect:' The Intimate Public of Personal Mommy Blogging," *Biography* 34.1 (Winter 2011): 37–8.
35. Lori Kido Lopez, 744.
36. Wilson and Yochim, "Pinning Happiness: Affect, Social Media, and the Work of Mothers," in *Cupcakes, Pinterest, Ladyporn: Feminized Popular Culture in the Early 21st century*. Ed. Elana Levine (Urbana, IL: University of Illinois Press, 2015), 232–48.
37. Aimée Morrison, "'Suffused by Feeling and Affect': The Intimate Public of Personal Mommy Blogging," *Biography* 34.1 (Winter 2011): 37–8.
38. Alison Trope, "Mother Angelina: Hollywood Philanthropy Personified," in *Commodity Activism*, 164.
39. "Draper James Gives Back," Draper James. Available online at www.draperjames.com/draper-james-gives-back/ (accessed February 9, 2016).
40. Jessica Alba, "Why I Started the Honest Company," *Huffington Post*, February 25, 2012. Available online at www.huffingtonpost.com/jessica-alba/the-honest-company_b_1300436.html (accessed December 9, 2014).
41. Roopali Mukherjee and Sarah Banet-Weiser, eds., *Commodity Activism: Cultural Resistance in Neoliberal Times* (New York: NYU Press, 2012).
42. "Behind the Scenes of the Honest Company with Jessica Alba," YouTube July 24, 2012. Available online at www.youtube.com/watch?v=Y_oMSmp44IU (accessed January 12, 2016); Clare O'Connor, "How Jessica Alba Built a $1 Billion Company, and a $200 Million Fortune, Selling Parents Peace of Mind, *Forbes*, June 15, 2015. Available online at www.forbes.com/sites/clareoconnor/2015/05/27/how-jessica-alba-built-a-1-billion-company-and-200-million-fortune-selling-parents-peace-of-mind/ (accessed April 10, 2016).
43. Mary C. Beltrán, "The Hollywood Latina Body as Site of Social Struggle: Media Constructions of Stardom and Jennifer Lopez's 'Cross-Over Butt,'" *Quarterly Review of Film & Video* 19: 2002, 72. See also Richard Dyer, *Heavenly Bodies: Film Stars and Society*, 2nd Edition (London: Routledge, 2004).
44. Mary Beltrán, *Latina/o Stars in U.S. Eyes: The Making and Meanings of Film and TV Stardom* (Urbana and Chicago: University of Illinois Press, 2009), 166.
45. Negra, *Off-White Hollywood: American Culture and Ethnic Female Stardom* (New York: Routledge, 2001), 138.
46. Beltrán, "The Hollywood Latina Body" 73.
47. Negra is referring in this quotation to Marisa Tomei's ethnically marked Italian American stardom. I extend her assertion to Alba's Mexican American celebrity. Negra, *Off-White Hollywood*, 145.
48. Ibid, 139–40.
49. Jessica Alba, *The Honest Life: Living Naturally and True to You* (New York: Rodale Books, 2013); Allison Takeda, "Jessica Alba: My Book Is 'More Grounded' than Gwyneth Paltrow's because 'I Didn't Grow Up with a Bunch of Money,' *Us Weekly* March 20, 2013. Available online at www.usmagazine.com/celebrity-moms/news/jessica-alba-my-book-is-more-grounded-than-gwyneth-paltrows-because-i-didnt-grow-up-with-a-bunch-of-money-2013203 (accessed April 10, 2016).
50. Alice Marwick and danah boyd, "To See and Be Seen: Celebrity Practice on Twitter," *Convergence* 17.2 (2011): 138–59.

4 TLC's Religious Moms
Branding Motherhood with Faith

In season five (2014) of their hit docusoap *Sister Wives* (TLC, 2008–), Meri, Christine, Janelle, and Robyn Brown, Kody Brown's four plural wives, launched an online lifestyle retailer called My Sisterwife's Closet. It was to be the middle-American mom's answer to the posh celebrity outlets like GOOP and Draper James, aspiring perhaps to the multi-platform, multi-product success of reality stars like Bethenny Frankel.[1] To fund the fledgling business, they sought investment from a venture capital firm run by a friend of Kody's.[2] After asking for $2.5 million, they received backing of $250,000; the vastly reduced sum illustrates recession-tightened budgets, but also the Brown wives' amateurish planning and presentations. In confessional interview segments, the wives describe being embarrassed by their lack of preparation for meetings, yet surprised that their formal pitch was interpreted as unprofessional by the potential investors. During the investor meeting, the Brown wives studiously avoided mentioning their reality show, even when questioned about where all their site visitors were coming from.[3] Masking the labor of performing reality TV is common, but in this context it reads as ignorance of the brand economy in which the family is attempting to function, or at best, an inability to recognize and capitalize on a branding advantage. Rather than a fatal flaw, however, the Brown wives' apparent lack of business acumen actually contributes to their almost aggressive normativity. It works to form an affective bond with middle-class consumers faced with recession and a cultural and political climate telling them they need to fend for themselves, and that the family, not the state, is the primary locus of financial and emotional support and safety. The inability to perform as polished, family-branded entrepreneurs speaks to their class position but also creates a sense of aww shucks nostalgia for pre-brand culture, pre-Internet, pre-feminist America that it shares with the TLC network's other megafamily hit *19 Kids and Counting* (2008–15). Ironically, despite the anti-feminist rhetoric and patriarchal structures embedded in their families, their reality programs, and the fringe religious faiths to which each cast adheres, the mothers are the stars of the show, the carriers of the family brand identity, and ultimately responsible for the financial as well as emotional well-being of their families.

As a counterpoint to previous chapters' focus on wealthy, urban, style-conscious women operating brands embedded in postfeminist discourses of fashion, beauty, body discipline, and household goods, this chapter offers an exploration of the function of conservative, middle-class, white, religious motherhood in contemporary reality TV and brand culture. These programs are in conversation with the same social, economic, and political contexts that form the backdrop for the entire book: mommy culture, recession, and increasingly visible inequalities of gender, race, and income. In contrast to the postfeminist negotiations performed by the wealthy women in earlier chapters though, the mothers at the center of these family narratives, by prodigious reproduction, create an imagined, conservative, all white pre-feminist America in the face of contemporary political battles around immigration, women's rights to control their own bodies, and LGBT and African American civil rights.

A Different Kind of Mommy Culture

I began this book by describing the contemporary twenty-first century version of an idealized, heroic mother: a peculiarly detailed image of a valiant mother who is loving, compassionate, and entirely and exclusively devoted to her children. This imagined mother, the central figure of what Susan Douglas and Meredith Michaels labeled "new momism" is utterly self-sacrificing and completely fulfilled by the intense emotional labor of this style of motherhood. This fantastical mother is also deeply political while being represented as totally outside politics. Her idealized image is imbricated in brand culture, discourses of postfeminism, and recession, and she is repeatedly invoked to create an idealized image of nation. Previous chapters have analyzed the ways in which celebrity women and their pregnancies, children (seen and unseen), and self-branded companies continuously shore up this celebrated notion of maternity while firmly reinforcing its aged, raced, and classed boundaries. This chapter pivots to explore a different facet of "mommy culture," the less aspirational, assertively middle-class, middle-of-the-country mothers on the TLC network's megafamily shows *Sister Wives* (2010–) and *19 Kids and Counting* (2008–15). Through the shows' low-budget realist aesthetics, their network brand, and the families' religious identities, *Sister Wives*' Brown family and *19 Kids*' Duggar family offer an alternative version of mommy culture just as bounded as those already discussed, but rooted in more socially and politically conservative modes of privilege. Their religious faith and rural or suburban locations activate myths of the American heartland and mobilize motherhood and brand culture in a different register than the more affluent, more secular, and much less reproductive women in earlier chapters. First, I discuss the family brands that put mothers at the center of narratives but subordinate their work to patriarchal family structures. Next, I explain the ways in which these two families' fringe religious identities operate as an anti- rather than postfeminist version of retreatism. From there, I link TLC's brand and its network aesthetics to these conservative representations, and finally, I conclude with a brief discussion of the 2015 Duggar sex scandal to explore the ideological gaps and cracks revealed when heroic motherhood fails.

Mothering Patriarchy

Sister Wives follows the aforementioned Browns, a polygamist Mormon family featuring the four wives Meri, Christine, Janelle, and Robyn, patriarch Kody, and their seventeen (going on eighteen as of this writing) children as they "come out" as a plural family, flee prosecution for polygamy in Utah, and subsequently build adjacent homes and start various businesses in Las Vegas, Nevada (in addition to My Sisterwife's Closet, one wife gets a real estate license; they consider opening a gym). *19 Kids and Counting* features the Duggar family, parents Jim Bob and Michelle, and their nineteen children, living in rural Arkansas. After several one-off specials, the show became a regular weekly series in 2008 and saw the family grow from seventeen to nineteen children before its cancellation. The oldest Duggar child, Joshua, married in 2008, and his wife and three children became part of the show as did the courtships, weddings, and children of the oldest Duggar daughters, Jessa and Jill.[4] Despite having such massive families-cum-ensemble casts and being firmly rooted in patriarchal religious cultures, both programs pivot around the mothers as the central characters and the carriers of the families' social and political identities as well as the architects and faces of the families' brands. It is Robyn, for example, who conceives My Sisterwife's Closet and refers to it as her "baby," and Michelle who is the primary author of the popular Duggar blogs and books as well as the most frequent authoritative voiceover heard on *19 Kids.*

The economic crisis that began in 2007–08 led to a radical increase in the visibility of a wide variety of inequalities from women's unequal access to reproductive health care and choice, to racial and economic disparities foregrounded by, for example, the election of Barack Obama, and protest movements like Black Lives Matter and Occupy. In that context, Rebecca Stephens argues that the extremely large families on *19 Kids and Counting* and *Sister Wives* speak to crucial social fears like "the recession's impact on gender roles, anxiety about dissolution of family, [and] fear of public intervention in private family life," and furthermore that they articulate contemporary cultural tensions including consumerism versus an inability or newly limited ability to consume, patriarchy versus feminism, new versus old models of marriage, and religion versus secularism.[5] Earlier chapters of this book have discussed the ways in which women's bodies and women's representations as mothers often stand in for political or nationalist discourses. Indeed, family size itself functions the same way, as Stephens highlights citing a 2012 Republican presidential debate in which the candidates all discussed their own family size: Rick Santorum, for whom the Duggars appeared at campaign events, has seven children; Michelle Bachmann is mother to five biological and twenty-three foster kids; and as an obstetrician, Ron Paul delivered some 4,000 babies.[6] Very large families in this context are shorthand for conservative political credentials. In *Sister Wives* and *19 Kids*, the burden of carrying excessive meaning still falls to central female characters, but these women are the architects of family brands rather than self-brands. Their labor in that regard can have the appearance of collectivity, sharing the burdens of representation, branding, and paid work among wives or generations of a family. This has the radical potential, as Brenda Weber notes, to foreground domestic and affective work-sharing and female collectivity, bucking the overwhelming dominance of neoliberalist discourses in reality TV. Unfortunately, this labor, even when shared among women, puts plainly gendered women's labor firmly in service of clearly articulated patriarchal family structures.

Like the enormous families on *Sister Wives* and *19 Kids*, actual household structures in the US in the early twenty-first century have shifted away from the (small) heteronormative family of mom, dad, and two or three children. Writing about nanny-to-the-rescue or parenting crisis programs, Ron Becker argues that their focus on the failure and reconstitution of the isolated nuclear family unit reflects anxiety on the part of those in power regarding those changing demographic trends. By showcasing families insulated in their suburban homes, this type of reality program idealizes the nuclear family, elevating those relationships above all others and reinforcing the idea that social networks or public services are not the proper way for Americans to find help and support.[7] The domestic settings and large numbers of children inevitably make *Sister Wives* and *19 Kids* shows about crisis parenting as well, and although they share the labor of household maintenance and child rearing among groups of women, the unusual family size keeps that labor contained within the nuclear family. The idea that American families must be self-contained, self-sufficient units and not rely on government benefits is explicit in the online viewer comments Rebecca Stephens examines that criticize the Duggars' "lack of control" for having so many children and the revelation by viewers of alleged bankruptcy filings by two of the Brown wives. Stephens documents viewers' resentment of helping support the Brown family by viewing *Sister Wives*, thereby participating in the market that keeps the show on the air and the Browns receiving appearance fees and an outlet for their brand identity, when the Browns have probably, according to commenters, "unfairly" used public funding in the past. Online commenters provide the voice of dominant neoliberal discourses via their dislike of participating in the Browns's inability to support their large family completely independently.[8] This resentment, however, is coupled with the shows' continued popularity. Furthermore, the investment of time and effort required to seek and share extratextual information about these families suggests negotiated viewing practices much like Bravo viewers'. If Bravo's "affluencers" tune in to ridicule the *Real Housewives* while still purchasing their branded products, *Sister Wives* and *19 Kids* cultivate a similarly contradictory viewing position.[9] These TLC viewers rail against the families' excesses and off-camera sins against the tightly contained, self-sufficient private families of the neoliberal ideal. Their continued viewership and even commitment to the shows, however, suggests the enduring appeal of the patriarchal family structures, middle-of-the-country locations, and reproduction of the white middle class via prolific child bearing encoded in the shows.

In a recreation of pre-feminist norms, these patriarchal family structures are maintained by the overvalued feminized labor of branding, household organization, and childcare. The wealthy reality performers and star-entrepreneurs in the rest of the book operated in a postfeminist mode, taking for granted feminist gains that provided them access to the workplace, but then founding businesses firmly within the feminized and disciplinary realms of fashion, beauty, and body maintenance. Postfeminism is notoriously difficult to define precisely, but one thing scholars agree on is that it assumes feminism accomplished its goals and is no longer necessary. The anti-feminism apparent on TLC's religious family shows assumes feminism accomplished its goals but understands that as a negative accomplishment. Thus, it mobilizes the choice rhetoric so common to postfeminist discourses and frames women's subordination to their husbands as a choice influenced by religious belief and morality. The mothers' position as the central figures of the shows, then, valorizes their subordination and frames it as a purposeful choice for women to perform the labor of reality performance, family-branding, and relationship maintenance in service of patriarchal family structures that very openly limit their authority.

On *Sister Wives*, for example, when My Sisterwife's Closet is represented as such an integral part of the five-way spousal relationship, the Browns attend a family therapy session for the cameras. During that session, Kody laments, "When have I ever been in charge of this family?" followed immediately by a cut to his explanation in a confessional interview: "Ultimately, somebody has to be the boss. Because my wives don't want to be subordinate to one another, I have to be the boss." In an interview segment following Kody's explanation, Meri corroborates by saying: "In a plural family, you should not have any one of the wives ruling, so to speak, over any of the other wives. For that reason, Robyn could never be CEO, as much as I would completely support her in being that."[10] In asserting that "someone has to be the boss," both Kody and Meri blithely dismiss the possibility of female collectivity (despite season-long representations of the wives working together, without Kody, to plan and launch the site) and place Kody in authority over the business venture. His outburst in therapy and these subsequent exchanges equate family relationships, family power structures, and family business; so Kody as CEO means Kody is head of home and family. Meri's comment represents the verisimilitude of feminism that has been "taken into account" by her insistence that she would support Robyn's leadership, but it simultaneously frames her and Robyn's retreat from a public leadership role as a purposeful choice on the part of women rather than a result of inflexible patriarchal power structures.[11]

All of this is further complicated, however, by the clear leadership of the women in these families who create and maintain the family brand. That Michelle and not her husband Jim Bob is given the show-defining authoritative voice over in the title sequence, for example, singles her out as the show's central axis and primary carrier of the family brand. Brenda Weber argues that *Sister Wives* is a potentially radical interrogation of family and gender roles, sharing the labor of being a wife and mother among four women instead of overburdening just one.[12] I would argue that the family brand storyline presents female leadership and entrepreneurship as possible even in an anti-feminist culture, but only as long as they function solely in support of male ambition and leadership. Thus, the dominance of brand culture, reliant as it is on feminized affective labor, works, at least in this instance, to reframe what could be feminist entrepreneurialism as active female support of patriarchy, a representational mode that has direct correlations to contemporary conservative politics.

Additionally, the focus on family over individual women has the effect not of foregrounding supportive familial networks of care and labor but of hiding the women's brand-work and entrepreneurialism and naturalizing the maternal labor that consumes so much screen time. TLC is not the only network to foreground family "as the locus of celebrity manufacture." The Kardashian family, according to Maria Pramaggiore and Diane Negra, "moves decidedly onto neoliberal turf, embracing privatization and market values, treating the family as a site of commercial productivity."[13] Like the Kardashians, the family is the primary site of ideological, celebrity, and commercial work for the Browns and the Duggars. The mothers are the central characters, stars, and embodiment of the brand, but very much unlike the female-headed and almost entirely female Kardashian family enterprise, the self-supporting nuclear family with the father as head is the hero of the Browns' and Duggars' narratives. In these programs, for the nuclear family to survive, traditionally gendered divisions of labor must be strictly maintained.

This situation is perhaps most obvious in the Duggar family's division of household chores into strictly delimited "jurisdictions," in which sons and daughters have completely separate, gender-specific lists of rotating household jobs. In a season one episode, the boys and girls swap chores and the girls learn to change a car tire and check the oil while the boys do laundry, cook, and clean the house. A producer asks Jill Duggar, one of the older daughters, why she and three of her sisters do most of the household cooking and cleaning. She explains that the four of them are older and better able to help and that "the boys do more of the outside manly work." When asked if she was reinforcing gender stereotypes by having girls cook and clean, Michelle voices a traditional anti-feminist position that there are inherent gender differences that lead the girls toward housework. The off-camera producer continues, asking if the Duggar daughters are being raised to be stay-at-home mothers. Michelle says no before launching into an explanation about how her daughters will inevitably choose that path because "that's their heart. They want to be married; they want to have a family and they want to allow their husband to have the role of being the main bread winner."[14] Michelle Duggar thus turns the institutionalization of her daughters into the gendered labor of private, domestic, unpaid housework and the ultimate goal of perpetuating that structure via heterosexual marriage, into a conscious choice. Moreover, in saying "it's their heart," she locates that choice in emotion, outside rational decision-making, reinforcing both the naturalization of the "choice," and the historical and anti-feminist association of women with emotion in contrast to men's rationality. In both programs, the feminized affective labor of mothering, relationship and brand management are the central foci, to the exclusion of paid public sphere work or more financialized forms of income. The feminized labor of brand management is incompatible with anti-feminist rhetoric and family structures that keep these mothers' onscreen labor focused on childcare and household management. Their unpolished and even unskilled brand production distinguishes these women from the postfeminist entrepreneurs whose fame and business acumen have taken feminism "into account." Their incapability in this realm, compared to their extreme competence managing very large families, reinforces the idea that women's skills operate best at home.

In the *19 Kids and Counting* title sequence, for example, Michelle explains in voice over that the Duggar family owns several commercial real estate properties, the income from which is their primary means of support. However, these properties do not become a filming location nor a plot point in the program. In fact, their mention in the credits seems calculated to prevent the kind of comments about out of control, unsupportable child bearing Stephens noted above. Aside from their mention in the opening titles and later a brief mention that the eldest Duggar son and his new wife will move into a rental property owned by his grandfather, this financialized form of income is erased from the onscreen narrative in favor of Michelle's frugality and her ability to lead the family in reusing, recycling, and making their own clothing, toys, and anything else possible. This type of domestic labor is in keeping with Emily Matchar's "new domesticity," and increasingly as the show's seasons multiply, the work of family branding and the sale of consumer products become part of this domestic and family labor.[15] Michelle writes books, maintains a blog on TLC.com, and makes public appearances to discuss parenting as well as stump for political candidates but the show is explicit that Jim Bob is the material and spiritual head of the family.[16] Women's labor, then, cannot be separated from patriarchal family structures, but is also tied to the patriarchal structures of the fringe religious sects to which these families belong, and those religious identities are an essential component of the family and even the network brands. Religious motherhood, then, is a branding mechanism for both family and network that helps create a distinctive picture of heroic motherhood in service of a right wing image of an ideal America away from liberal coastal areas, that is middle- or lower-middle-class, entrepreneurial, and is represented as having direct political efficacy.

TLC's Brand of Religion

The network that airs *19 Kids* and *Sister Wives* is TLC. Its unique brand identity works symbiotically with the Brown and Duggar family brands to promote a homogeneous image of conservative American cultural values across its programming. Despite having shed its original moniker, The Learning Channel, in favor of the stands-for-nothing acronym, TLC crafts a brand identity that draws on cultural functions of documentary and historic ties between reality TV and social science to create an educational ethos and emphasize the authenticity of its performers in contrast to other reality TV programs and brands. Denying the trashy reputation reality TV has now, many TLC shows strike an earnest tone that rejects the camp and style of the other female-centered reality TV shows and celebrity texts examined in this book. Instead, it self-consciously recalls early reality programming's documentary roots that can work to give its programming added cultural weight. Duggar meals, for example, are often accompanied by Michelle explaining how to prepare such vast quantities of food (particularly the fan favorite tater tot casserole) affordably. Michelle is also her children's home-school teacher, so we see her quite literally giving lessons on screen about the family's faith. Similarly, the Brown family frequently explains their religious beliefs in interview segments of their own show but also on morning chat shows and at various speaking engagements. They have been invited to speak to university students both on and off air, not about reality TV, but about their family structure and their "calling" to plural marriage.[17]

When reality television as we recognize it today started its path to ascendance in the 1990s, scholars worked to understand how this nonfictional genre was different from other nonfiction genres and definitions of documentary. John Corner called it "postdocumentary television," arguing that it does not fit any of the three classic cultural functions of documentary: the project of democratic civics, journalistic inquiry and exposition, or radical interrogation and alternative perspective.[18] On the contrary, however, Brenda Weber argues that it is actually the cultural understanding of reality TV as "low" or "trashy" that prevents viewers and critics from immediately recognizing those higher-order cultural functions. In fact, Weber singles out *Sister Wives*, with the affective and practical labor of being a wife and mother shared among four women, as an example of a show that might provide a radical interrogation or alternative perspective, to borrow Corner's words, of gender roles and family structures.[19] Both the Duggars and the Browns have also demonstrated real world political activism absent from the brand-centric or socially responsible business models observed in previous chapters. They engage with public solutions to the issues for which they advocate, and show government, not private enterprise or individual philanthropy, actually working for conservative causes. The Brown family's legal struggles, for example, have led to direct legislative change. They filed suit against the State of Utah in 2011 on the grounds that the anti-polygamy statutes used to drive them out of the state under fear of prosecution violated their right to privacy. In December 2014, a federal judge in the case ruled Utah's anti-polygamy laws unconstitutional.[20] The Duggars are also politically active. Patriarch Jim Bob is a former Arkansas state legislator, oldest son Josh was, until 2015, a lobbyist with the right wing Christian group the Family Research Council, and the family stumps for (extremely conservative) Republican candidates throughout the South and even farther afield. Michelle and Jim Bob have made appearances for Republicans from presidential hopeful Rick Santorum to Missouri Congressman Todd Akin (who, when asked if he supported access to abortion in the case of rape, notoriously said that in cases of "legitimate rape, the female body has ways to try to shut the whole thing down") among others.[21] This kind of visible direct efficacy is absent from this book's other case studies. Alarmingly then, the only time the state visibly acts in relation to mothers held up as heroes or celebrities is to legalize polygamy and elect male politicians in favor of denying women access to health care and enforcing mandatory maternity. So, via TLC's network brand and its individual programs, we begin to see how these mothers' affective and branding labor is inextricable from religion, region, and an anti- rather than postfeminist culture.

Religious motivation and the tight links between conservative religious rhetoric and right wing politics are common features among these families, their political activities, and the network brand. If the family is the locus of all modes of labor on *Sister Wives* and *19 Kids*, religion makes these families distinct enough to become television programs, and, as television characters, religion becomes the linchpin of their identity. For many of the TLC network's reality families, the spectacle required to transform a family into a reality cast comes from their religions' fringe status, conservatism, and espoused desire to protect and separate their children from mainstream popular culture. The strict conservative social values they voice include patriarchal family structures, insistence on modesty (primarily for girls and women), sexual abstinence, and firmly gendered divisions of labor with a strong emphasis on childbearing and childcare for women and girls, in addition to the maintenance of the family brand.

The TLC network mobilizes these fringe religions as part of its brand identity, creating an earnest middle-class address that, in part, aligns religion with a notion of "real America" geographically rooted to the middle of the country and essential to conservative political responses to the multiple crises threatening any unified idea of an American nation in the early twenty-first century. Rather than parade these conservative faiths as a sort of "freak show," as some have maintained, I argue that TLC uses its more educational mode to present fringe religions (as long as they are Christian or have ties to Protestant Christianity) as modes of difference that are assimilable into dominant middle-class whiteness that, in turn, reinforces the fiction of a unified middle-class in the so-called American heartland. Because family size, gendered labor, and female centrality are such important components of these shows, motherhood once again carries a large part of that representational burden.

Motherhood creates meaning on the TLC religious family shows in two interrelated ways, in addition to its narrative centrality: through family size and an insistence on "natural" motherhood. The latter not only reinforces the common postfeminist trope that motherhood is the only path to complete fulfilled selfhood for women, but it also distances these mothers from their implied opposite. These TLC mothers do not go in for the medical intervention we saw in Chapter One, nor are they excessive, absent, or embarrassing mothers as in Chapter Two. Instead, motherhood and the middle-classness that put those treatments and behaviors out of reach are not just normalized but held up as the only correct path to maternity and therefore complete selfhood for women. We see explicit examples of this on both *19 Kids* and *Sister Wives*. During the opening titles of *19 Kids*, for example, Michelle Duggar provides the explanatory and authoritative voice over introductions to her family and their beliefs. This title sequence, which changed only slightly over the show's long run, always included Michelle saying, "That's a grand total of 19 [kids], and I delivered every one of them." This statement emphasizes Michelle's motherhood as biological and embodied. It also coheres with the Duggars's religious beliefs, which ban contraception and encourage couples to have as many children as God will provide, thus emphasizing a supposed naturalness to motherhood and extremely large, unplanned families. Similarly, Meri Brown's struggles to conceive on *Sister Wives*, and her self-perception as less of a woman and a less equal wife for having contributed only one child to the family, also operate to foreground "natural" motherhood as these reality performers' central characteristic and the only proper path to maternity. We see this foregrounding of natural motherhood, in particular, when Kody discourages her from accepting Robyn's offer to act as a surrogate. This direct contrast to Giuliana Rancic's use of a gestational carrier discussed in Chapter One reflects the different modes of heroic white motherhood for the wealthy, liberal, and urban, rendered less "natural" by their age, the medical intervention they require to become mothers, and by implication their careerism, versus the middle-class, conservative, and rural. Thus, in these conservative family shows, motherhood is not only mandated as the only path to fulfillment for women but it also frames excessively reproductive middle-class mothers as more authentic than the wealthy women on other shows, a theme that continues in the network's brand aesthetic.

Natural motherhood is thus valorized, but strictly classed, which is part of TLC's brand of conservative middle-Americanness. TLC programs carefully police representations and performances of class, a representational practice that has led to its frequent characterization not as a "quality reality" TV outlet but as a modern freak show.[22] Indeed, some of TLC's programming, notably *Here Comes Honey Boo Boo* (2012–14), one of its biggest hits before its cancellation amid controversy in 2014, and others like *My Crazy Obsession* (2012–)[23] seem closer to "the twenty-first century version of the freak shows of the past" than to any educational or documentary roots the genre might claim.[24] Programs like *Honey Boo Boo* and *Crazy Obsession* spectacularize bodies and behaviors that are represented as unfit in order to reinforce "myriad stereotypes about gender, race, and class while seeming to celebrate spectacular cultural difference."[25] Class and religion are most often the factors that move a TLC show from the freak show to what I would call a more educational mode of reality. Characters framed as poor, or more importantly lacking entrepreneurial spirit evidenced by onscreen businesses and well-promoted family brands and products, and/or lacking conservative patriarchal "family values," like Honey Boo Boo's matriarchal clan, are overwhelmingly portrayed "freakishly," while entrepreneurs and characters who perform middle-class identities are framed as opportunities to learn.

My Big Fat American Gypsy Wedding (2012–), for example, is a format imported from British Channel 4 (*Big Fat Gypsy Weddings* 2010–) where it began as a one-off program billed as a documentary. The British original, from which the American pilot episode is almost an exact copy relocated to the US, provided cultural information about and interviews with Traveller (the preferred term to the pejorative Gypsy) communities in Britain. These interviews and voice over narration served to recuperate courting and wedding rituals into standard working-class nuclear family structures. At the same time, the hushed tone of the off-screen narrator throughout brought with it condescension and a voyeuristic ethnographic gaze that clearly positioned Traveller culture as outside the norm, and "incit[ed] moral outrage" in the mode of the freak show.[26] These patterns were repeated mostly whole cloth in the American program and, to a slightly lesser extent, on its West Virginia-set spin-off series *Gypsy Sisters* (2013–). *Breaking Amish* (2012–), another popular TLC show, similarly treads a middle ground, portraying the young people choosing to leave Amish and Mennonite faith communities sympathetically, but often framing the families they have left behind as bizarre, unreasonable, or, ironically, as crassly fame-seeking.

Rebecca Stephens maintains that religion is the primary means of "othering" families that otherwise represent the dominant; I would argue, however, that this othering does not necessarily play on the fear that what looks like "us" might really be "them," as she puts it.[27] Rather, these main characters' religious identities work as "family values" that attempt to normalize communities initially framed as outsiders into white middle-class or lower-middle-class norms. On *Breaking Amish*, the young women (and men) maintain their faith and conservative values but are mainstreamed from their segregated communities into what they call the "English" world.

These recuperation narratives reaffirm the "normalcy" of conservative middle-class whiteness and add Christian[28] religion to the understanding of "normalcy." Within this brand identity, far from inciting moral outrage, multiple wives, for example, function instead to illustrate the utmost importance of the nuclear family as the ultimate site of economic labor and physical and emotional care, which is already normalized within reality TV's neoliberal governmentality. In the same vein, Tanya Zuk argues that *Sister Wives'* educational project is part of a mission to "assimilate" fundamentalist Mormonism and polygamy into mainstream American culture. She writes that "Kody and his family strive to normalize suburban polygamy, particularly as *Sister Wives* equates the difference between the LDS and FLDS Mormons to the Protestant Reformation and minimizes the religious aspects of 'the lifestyle' of polygamy."[29] While I doubt polygamy will become mainstream in American culture any time soon, Zuk's assessment of the Browns' use of pedagogical rhetoric and the language of lifestyling to normalize their family structure is spot on and works well with the earnest element of TLC's brand.

It is important to note in this context the overwhelming whiteness of TLC's serial reality programs.[30] Certain registers of difference, such as ability and religion, are normalized within a conservative, middle-class whiteness, offering the appearance of inclusivity while reinscribing conservative social and economic values that, in fact, actively exclude or discriminate against people of color.[31] The fringe religious identities of many of TLC's reality performers fall into this category. They do not serve to spectacularize the performers' bodies or lifestyles the way Honey Boo Boo and her family are seen to revel in the grotesqueness of their bodily functions. Insistence on modest dress and no sex—or even hand holding, for the Duggars—before marriage, in fact, aggressively de-spectacularizes the bodies on *Sister Wives*, *19 Kids*, and some of TLC's other religion-focused programs, keeping the narrative focus squarely on stories of mothering and branding labor.

Sarah Banet-Weiser argues that rather than simply applying market logics to faith products, religious brands "are positioned as a *response*—even a challenge—to advanced capitalism."[32] There is an interesting, almost anti-capitalist, implicit rejection of the decadence of coastal elites and the reality TV women who represent them in TLC's religious family-branded shows. But rather than actually challenge capitalism, they more insidiously mask neoliberal capitalism in the guise of massive families-cum-communities and ham-fisted attempts at family branding. The Brown family's online jewelry venture seems to be set up in precisely this fashion. Its relative lack of success and its inability to convert millions of website hits to comparable sales numbers demonstrate an incompatibility between a religiously marked heartland family and success in a contemporary brand economy that equates sales with the fulfillment of the self. The Browns are participating in a precarious economy in the neoliberal entrepreneurial mode endorsed by the political right, but their failure threatens both the family and its economic stability.

Meri, Christine, Janelle, and Robyn pursue a number of money-making opportunities from Janelle earning her real estate license to the family's ultimately unrealized attempts to open a fitness center. The venture with the most prominent place in the show's narrative, however, is My Sisterwife's Closet, the consumer products brand that mimics the promotion of self-branded products we have seen on other programs. Whereas *Real Housewives of New York* Ramona Singer's or Sonja Morgan's branding missteps (see Chapter Two) show them up as too old for postfeminist mommy culture, here the Browns' branding missteps help recuperate or reinforce their normalcy—they are learning to function in this new economy just like us viewers. It is the family's relative failure to capitalize on their reality TV notoriety, their inability to create a lucrative consumer products brand, that marks them as "other," and highlights their inability to integrate into postfeminist brand culture in much the same way that age marks Singer and Morgan as unfit or unruly. But rather than highlight them as unfit postfeminist subjects in the manner of the too-old *Housewives*, this ineptness reinforces their averageness. They struggle financially "just like us" and are thus recuperated not into postfeminism, but into a necessarily anti-feminist Middle America.

TLC's Brand: An Aesthetics of Conservatism

Pierre Bourdieu tells us that taste is a function of class, and on TLC, aesthetics are not only classed but visualize social and political ideologies. In this case, the network's aesthetics clearly endorse the conservative middle-class or lower-middle-classes as contrasting and ostensibly superior to the liberal, affluent, and aspirational aesthetics on Bravo.[33] On US television, Bravo and TLC are the two channels that program nearly exclusively reality and, furthermore, nearly exclusively female-centered docusoaps. So they are a realm in which women, mostly mothers, and their reproductive bodies, carry political burdens through stylistic and melodramatic excess as on Bravo or reproductive and marital excess on TLC. The lower-budget, more realist aesthetic of TLC's brand of reality TV creates a sense of immediacy and naturalness that mirrors the rhetoric of natural, embodied motherhood evident on two of its most popular shows. All these links to the "real" and evocations of the "natural" create the idea that the images onscreen are "normal." That is, thanks to reality TV's governmentality, plus the cultural heft of this documentary or educational feeling, it can seem like TLC's families represent the "right" way to be American. And that particular right way is white, religious, socially conservative, and enormously reproductive.

TLC's more realist aesthetic includes occasional visible "mistakes," like boom microphones and even the occasional crewmember entering the frame, echoing a cultivated amateurishness similar to the Brown wives' attempts to raise money for My Sisterwife's Closet. TLC crafts its own brand aesthetic with a tendency toward de-saturated color palettes (a stark contrast, for example, to Bravo's bright bubble gum palette), and filming locations that favor suburban or rural areas, often in the American South, West, or Midwest, away from the liberal enclaves of the coasts. This aesthetic extends to the makeup, hairstyles, wardrobes, and even home design of its characters, which we can see clearly in both *Sister Wives* and *19 Kids*.

In two starkly contrasted promotional images, the New York *Real Housewives* wear elegant cocktail dresses, stiletto heels, and hold hands on cocked hips in typical red carpet poses. They are all slender and heavily made up. The accompanying graphics illustrate cocktails, high-end retail destination 5th Avenue, and the word "socialite." In contrast, the Brown family, even while wearing similarly jewel-toned shirts, stand in front of a drab blue backdrop. They all wear trousers; only Robyn is particularly slim. They stand as though in a family snapshot, directly facing the camera. While their hair and makeup are almost certainly professionally done, it is much subtler, chasing the "natural look" or a certain suburban chic rather than the fashion and sophistication cultivated in the Bravo cast photo. In a similar promotional image, the enormous Duggar family poses in its entirety in front of the family home on a huge expanse of lawn that is part of their property and evokes the more rural Arkansas setting. In this image, the entire family wears matching khaki trousers or long skirts and pastel-colored shirts that evoke a church picnic more than the opulence the *Housewives* embody. The size of the Duggar family and their matching outfits are designed to emphasize the family unit, rather than individuals, but if we look closer, we can see that Michelle and her daughters typically wear little makeup and do not have their hair professionally straightened or styled. Furthermore, on the show, Michelle often discusses thrift shopping, reusing, and making her family's clothing, which is directly in keeping with this lower-budget, more realist aesthetic.

We are introduced to the Brown family in their home in Lehi, Utah, a suburb of Provo (and less than 20 miles from suburban Sandy where HBO's polygamist soap opera *Big Love* [2006–11], the inspiration for *Sister Wives*, was set). According to one commentator, Madeleine Schwartz, "From the outside [the Brown home] appears boxy and drab, like a cheap attempt at a McMansion. It is not much to look at."[34] She goes on to note that the banal exterior conceals a rather remarkable sprawling home that contains three separate apartments for Kody Brown's then three wives (one first season storyline was the entrance of fourth wife Robyn into the family). For Schwartz, the house represents a metaphor; the interior and the unusual family it houses serve as evidence of changing family structures in the US, but they are contained within a strictly patriarchal package that is as ugly and old fashioned as the home's exterior. This metaphor is a little labored, but the home's banality, equaled really by the actual side-by-side tract homes or "McMansions" in a suburban Las Vegas cul-de-sac where the family moves in later seasons, immediately normalizes the Brown family, and situates them firmly in an imagined middle America. The contrast between the Browns' home, the Duggars' sprawling but otherwise un-noteworthy abode in rural Alabama, and the massive and over-designed luxury homes and urban locales of Bravo's *Real Housewives* is substantial. If homes with such a mass-produced look as the Browns' recall the trauma of economic crisis, they are also homes recognizable almost anywhere in the country. Coupled with Utah's mountain vistas or the trees and fields that surround the Duggars' home—big enough that neighbors are never visible and for the Duggar children to cruise around off-road style in the family pick-up truck when they are learning to drive—these filming locations evoke the vast middle, the largely conservative rural and suburban audiences not valued by entertainment industrial and critical notions of profitable 'quality' audiences. What they do evoke is a sense of "real" middle America planting a popular culture foothold against the coastal locations and urban populations that dominate representation and provide programmers with affluent "quality" audiences.

The Duggar and Brown families, in partnership with TLC, use their religious identities as well as their geographical locations as shorthand markers of wholesome averageness, and conservative Americanness; they work as a "hyperbolic normativity" that sets them apart from the excessive consumption and excessive femininity of reality celebrities like the Kardashians or the *Real Housewives*.[35] It is essential to note that the programs and brands analyzed in this book have all either been launched or sustained popularity through a period of economic disaster and constant reminders of growing inequality and social upheaval on a national and even international scale. If it is the ideological work of mainstream entertainment to shore up the status quo, the Duggars and Browns seem perfectly suited to teaching families to circle the wagons and support themselves via thrift and entrepreneurial spirit, thereby dispelling any need or desire to participate in the steady stream of collective protest movements gaining broad public notice in the 2010s.

TLC's religious families offer a sense that the "real America" not only still has a popular culture presence but can also be a bulwark against incursions on the sanctity of both the nuclear family and the national family. This perception is also reflected in the network's less polished aesthetics and emphasis on the conservative, hetero-family-centric ideologies that dominate the network and the basically exclusive presentation of hardworking, middle-class, and geographically central "Real Americans." The phrase "real America," was popularized by Sarah Palin during her 2008 Vice Presidential candidacy to describe her working-class, rural conservative base in contrast to the out-of-touch elites in Washington and liberal coastal cities.[36] Palin's bid for the second highest office in the land obviously failed, but her bid for reality celebrity was much more successful as she became a Fox News pundit and the star of her own 8-episode TLC mini-series, *Sarah Palin's*

Alaska (2010–11). Laurie Ouellette describes Palin's media success within the logics of cable television narrowcasting and brand culture. Narrowcasting, she writes,

> assumes that consumers are deeply divided by lifestyle and taste.... Something similar has happened with political culture, when differences steeped in class, region, race, gender, and generation, as well as party membership, are mapped onto taste cultures and consumer markets.

Palin's branded self relies on her working-class accent, her questionable grammar (something she shared with George W. Bush's folksy Texan persona), and her performance of rugged self-reliance in relation to the Alaskan wilderness.[37] A plethora of reality shows like *Deadliest Catch* (Discovery 2005–), *Gold Rush Alaska* (Discovery 2010–14), and *Ice Road Truckers* (History 2007–13), to name a few, feature these same types of performances, but typically of a frontier masculinity under economic threat and out of place in gentrified urban settings.[38] Ouellette mentions Palin's favorite self-descriptions "mama grizzly" and "hockey mom," but does not emphasize the essential role that constant reminders of her heroic motherhood of five children, one of whom has special needs, played in crafting her persona and forging the necessary affective bonds with viewers and voters for an effective personal brand. Replacing Alaska with rural Alabama or suburban Utah and Nevada, this same style shapes the Browns' and Duggars' mother-driven family-brands. Jim Bob Duggar's role is carefully segregated to masculinized activities outside the home, while the bulk of the show focuses on Michelle's household management. Similarly, the Brown wives are the central figures of their show, with Kody often bumbling as he moves from home to home, exerting authority but lacking anything to actually do in the domestic spaces that make up the bulk of the filming.

Victoria Johnson argues that images of the American "heartland" come to prominence "in times of cultural transition or perceived cultural threat or tension, [because] the heartland myth provides a short-hand cultural common sense framework for 'all-American' identification, [and] redeeming goodness."[39] Both the Browns and the Duggars eagerly play into this heartland myth, not just with their locations, but also with their dress, speech, and choice of products to create and sell. Both families dress modestly, which means girls cover their shoulders and knees and never show cleavage (boys have no specific restrictions). They are essentially the template for the "stylized blandness" hip urbanites have labeled Normcore.[40] Far more than a fashion punchline though, like the shows' locations, the modest and inexpensive clothing evokes a heartland ethos also visible in the shows' aesthetics. Regardless of realities, Heartland, rural, and conservative are all coded as white in American culture and it is impossible to understand the Duggars' reproductive excesses outside the context of the anti-abortion policies for which they campaign. As I detailed in the introduction, those policies disproportionately affect women of color, stigmatizing them and their children as unruly, unwanted, and deviant. Just as the expensive, difficult to conceive babies in Chapter One create heroic white mothers in contrast to the denigrated pregnancies of ethnically marked celebrities or tabloid personalities (like Nadya Suleman and Kim Kardashian), so the sheer quantity of white children on TLC's religious mega family shows seem to form a phalanx of whiteness against anyone seeking equal rights. This is only reinforced by the near total absence of people of color on TLC. People of color appear regularly on the network's ecumenical Friday Bride Day programming block, but rarely anywhere else in the channel's lineup. The aggressive normativity and push to recuperate so many discourses of difference written on white bodies into a dominant middle-Americanness only highlights who is excluded: anyone non-heterosexual and any people of color. As throughout the book, we see white mothers, this time primarily through sheer quantity of children, creating an image of an idealized family and an idealized nation, this time from a conservative perspective: middle-class, middle-of-the-country, Christian families working as isolated, self-supporting economic units.

A Duggar Scandal: When Heartland Motherhood Fails

I began this chapter by telling the story of My Sisterwife's Closet, the struggling online retail outlet of the *Sister Wives* Brown family. In that story, I argued, the Brown family's amateurish and only moderately successful bid for venture capital actually supported their strident averageness, their middle-class, middle-American brand, and their conservative aesthetic. The ways the Brown parents try to keep their kids away from contemporary popular culture they understand as immoral and, in particular, hypersexual is mirrored in their inability to capitalize on their name recognition on the Internet. In other words, the Internet is the home and the symbol of worldly popular culture to which the Brown parents Meri, Janelle, Christine, Robyn, and Kody, are opposed (albeit mildly compared to the Duggars). So, it makes sense that they are not very good at making a business work that requires them to exploit that technology. Furthermore, they are specifically incapable of transforming millions of site visitors into actual consumers. They have failed, in fact, not just in understanding what products their viewers might want and by extension who their viewers are but they have also failed at sustaining and spreading a family brand from TV to a new platform, to create their own "transmediated continuity." They have failed to thrive within brand culture. This chapter concludes by examining another such failure.

In 2015, *In Touch Weekly*, primarily a celebrity gossip tabloid, broke news of a Duggar family scandal that eventually dismantled the Duggar brand empire.[41] Josh Duggar, the oldest child and as of this writing a father of three in his own right, was accused of "improperly touching" five girls, at least two of whom were his sisters, when he was 14 or 15 years old.[42] TLC immediately stopped airing reruns of the series and canceled the show shortly thereafter. Meanwhile, Josh Duggar resigned from his post at the Family Research Council, a conservative Christian lobbying group in Washington, DC, and his family began giving interviews to minimize the scandal, apologize, and protect the brand. Notably, this apology tour features not the remorseful alleged perpetrator, who was kept out of sight, but his parents and sisters. As we have observed throughout this chapter, in contradiction to the strict patriarchal family structures espoused on these religious family docusoaps, it is the women who develop, maintain, and embody the family brands. The affective nature of brand work, after all, mimics the affective labor of mothering. Both require the building and maintaining of strong emotional bonds and within a mother-obsessed cultural moment, both facilitate the eventual sale of products and economic gain.

This scandal, however, strikes at the heart of the Duggars' nostalgic, heartland, family-centered brand. During courting or dating, the Duggars require a couple to be chaperoned at all times and disallow all touch except "side hugs" before marriage. Even hand holding happens for the first time on the wedding day. In the *19 Kids and Counting* world, sexuality is on constant display via Michelle and her older daughters' continual pregnancies but it is also always framed as a threat. It can only be safely expressed in one way: heterosexual marriage and the reproduction of the family economic unit. But since *19 Kids* has been canceled as a result of this scandal, Michelle and Jim Bob, without the constantly reinforced name recognition and wholesome conservative family brand, will lose their invitations to speak at political rallies. Josh has already stepped down from his political position. The TLC-sponsored blogs and recipes Michelle maintains will be archived or will disappear. The imagined America the Duggars' show and much of the TLC brand conjures will be more intensely challenged than it typically is.

The scandal hinges on deviant, out-of-control sexuality. This is an obvious disruption of the arch conservative Duggar brand and so many of the conservative family brands on the TLC network that insist sexuality can only be expressed via reproduction within a heterosexual marriage. Arguably, the reasons the scandal was unrecoverable, despite the female-driven apology tour, were economic recovery and the undeniable threat to the Duggar family's "hyperbolic normativity" the scandal represented. By 2015, the US economy had mostly righted itself after the collapse of 2008. For women, the focus on domesticity as a response to not having access to the workplace was growing less urgent and shifting toward access to employment and pay equity. The thrift and make-do mentality that Michelle and the rest of the Duggars peddled starting in 2008 were less relevant. The second factor brings us back to motherhood and the ways in which, for the Duggar brand and TLC, sexuality was only allowable in the service of reproducing the conservative vision of a middle-class white family; an imagined family that could withstand cultural pressure to redefine marriage as more inclusive, to enforce the civil rights of immigrants and people of color, and most immediately, to allow all women equal access to reproductive health care and choice. The scandal disrupted the idea that the Duggars were a simple educational voice and replaced the aesthetics of conservatism with the aesthetics of scandal: tearful interviews, appearances on news specials instead of bubbly morning chat shows, and tabloid covers that screamed "Josh Duggar Chilling Molestation Confession in New Police Report" rather than special issues devoted to Jessa and Jill's weddings.[43] This break in the family's brand aesthetic and the ideology it represented was the unrecoverable rupture. It is this failure, the crack in the brand and the covalent crack in the ideology of postfeminist mommy culture supported and perpetuated by this particular brand, that I explore in the concluding chapter.

Notes

1. GOOP and Draper James are Gwyneth Paltrow's and Reese Witherspoon's respective lifestyle sites (see Chapter Three). Bethenny Frankel, sometime star of *The Real Housewives of New York*, has parlayed her reality fame into enormous financial gain with Skinnygirl, her brand of low-calorie cocktails, subsequently sold to Jack Daniel's. For a detailed analysis of Frankel's fame and the labor behind her self-branded success, see Suzanne Leonard and Diane Negra, "After Ever After: Bethenny Frankel, Self-Branding, and the 'New Intimacy of Work,'" in *Cupcakes, Pinterest, and Ladyporn: Feminized Popular Culture in the Early Twenty-First Century*, ed. Elana Levine, (Urbana: University of Illinois Press, 2015).
2. I use first names throughout this chapter because so many performers share the same last name.
3. Even their estimate of the site's web traffic is unprofessional; Christine cites the enormous range of 2–15 million users. "Polygamists in a Shark Tank." *Sister Wives* 5.2, TLC, Originally aired June 15, 2014.
4. Josh Duggar was also the subject of a sexual scandal that led to the show's cancellation in 2015. I discuss that scandal in the conclusion to this chapter.
5. Rebecca Stephens, "Supersizing the Family: Nation, Gender, and Recession on Reality TV," *Reality Gendervision: Sexuality and Gender on Transatlantic Reality Television*, ed. Brenda Weber, (Durham, NC: Duke University Press, 2014), 170.
6. Stephens, 184.
7. Becker situates these shows specifically in the context of increasing acceptance and legalization of same sex marriage before it was legalized nationally by the US Supreme Court. Ron Becker, "'Help Is on the Way!': *Supernanny, Nanny 911* and the Neoliberal Politics of the Family," in *The Great American Makeover: Television, History, Nation*, ed. Dana Heller, (New York: Palgrave-Macmillan, 2006), 175–191.
8. Stephens, 179.
9. Affluencers.com, Bravo's ad sales website (accessed May 29, 2013).
10. "Polygamists in a Shark Tank," *Sister Wives* 5.2, TLC, Originally aired June 15, 2014.
11. Angela McRobbie, "Postfeminism and Popular Culture," *Feminist Media Studies* 4.3 (2004): 255. McRobbie describes postfeminism as having taken feminism "into account."

12. Brenda Weber, "Trash Talk: The Gender Politics of Reality Television," *Reality Gendervisions: Sexuality and Gender on Transatlantic Reality TV*, ed. Brenda Weber, (Durham, NC: Duke University Press, 2014), 1–34.

13. Maria Pramaggiore and Diane Negra, "Keeping Up with the Aspiration: Commercial Family Values and the Kardashian Brand," *Reality Gendervision: Sexuality and Gender on Transatlantic Reality Television*, ed. Brenda Weber, (Durham, NC: Duke University Press, 2014), 87, 89.

14. "Trading Places, Duggar Style," *17 Kids and Counting* 1.8, TLC, Originally aired October 27, 2008.

15. Emily Matchar, *Homeward Bound: Why Women Are Embracing the New Domesticity*, (New York: Simon & Schuster, 2013), Kindle Edition.

16. Stephens, 170.

17. Danielle Tumminio, "My Take: Why This Female Priest Loves *Sister Wives*," CNN Belief Blog, February 28, 2011. Available online at http://religion.blogs.cnn.com/2011/02/28/my-take-why-this-female-priest-loves-sister-wives/ (accessed April 11, 2016).

18. John Corner, "Performing the Real: Documentary Diversions," *Reality TV: Remaking Television Culture*, 2nd ed., eds. Susan Murray and Laurie Ouellette, (New York, New York University Press, 2009), 48–50.

19. Weber, "Trash Talk."

20. As of September 2014, Utah is appealing the ruling to the US 10th district Court of Appeals. Sarah Pulliam Bailey, "Utah Polygamy Court Ruling on 'Sister Wives' Case Confirms Fears of Social Conservatives." Religion News Service. Posted on *Huffington Post* (December 17, 2013). Available online at www.huffingtonpost.com/2013/12/17/utah-polygamy-court-ruling_n_4455706.html (accessed October 3, 2014); Brady McCombs, "Utah to Appeal Ruling in 'Sister Wives' Case," Associated Press, Posted on ABCNews.com. (accessed October 3, 2014.)

21. Lori Moore, "Rep. Todd Akin: The Statement and the Reaction," *New York Times* Politics blog, August 20, 2012. Available online at www.nytimes.com/2012/08/21/us/politics/rep-todd-akin-legitimate-rape-statement-and-reaction.html (accessed April 11, 2016); Rebecca Berg, "Duggar Family Joins Todd Akin's Campaign," *Buzzfeed* October 18, 2012. Available online at www.buzzfeed.com/rebeccaberg/duggar-family-joins-todd-akins-campaign (accessed April 11, 2016); Angela Duria, "Duggar Family Joins Rick Santorum on Campaign Trail in WI," *Fox6Now.com*. Available online at http://fox6now.com/2012/04/02/duggar-family-joins-rick-santorum-on-campaign-trail-in-wi/ (accessed April 11, 2016); Jenna Johnson and Jeremy Borden, "Stars of '19 Kids and Counting' Stump for Cuccinelli in Virginia," *Washington Post* October 16, 2013. Available online at www.washingtonpost.com/local/virginia-politics/2013/10/16/0653b77a-35eb-11e3-80c6-7e6dd8d22d8f_story.html (accessed April 11, 2016).

22. Jane Feuer, "'Quality' Reality and the Bravo Media Reality Series," *Camera Obscura* 30.1 (2015): 185–95.

23. *Here Comes Honey Boo Boo* follows *Toddlers and Tiaras* (2009–) fan favorite Alana "Honey Boo Boo" Thompson and her overweight, rural, working class family from one sassy catchphrase to the next, often relishing Alana's descriptions of every variety of bodily function. *My Crazy Obsession* does essentially what it says on the tin: each episode chronicles one person's obsessive collection. The first episode of the regular series, for example, features a couple who has

amassed over 5,000 Cabbage Patch Kids (ostensibly the largest collection in the world) to whom they speak and whose individual names they know, and one woman who must have absolutely everything, including her food, drink, and dog, pink. "5,000 kids & Tickled Pink," *My Crazy Obsession* 1.1 TLC, Originally aired March 7, 2012.

24. Rebecca Stephens, "Supersizing the Family: Nation, Gender, and Recession on Reality TV," *Reality Gendervision: Sexuality and Gender on Transatlantic Reality Television*, ed. Brenda Weber, (Durham, NC: Duke University Press, 2014), 176; see also Laura Backstrom, "From the Freak Show to the Living Room: Cultural Representations of Dwarfism and Obesity," *Sociological Forum* 27.3 (September 2012): 682–707; Kirsten Pike, "Freaky Five-Year-Olds and Mental Mommies: Narratives of Gender, Race and Class in TLC's *Toddlers & Tiaras*," *Reality Gendervision: Sexuality and Gender on Transatlantic Reality Television*, ed. Brenda Weber.

25. Pike, "Freaky Five-Year Olds," 283.

26. Tracey Jensen and Jessica Ringrose, "Sluts That Choose vs. Doormat Gypsies: Exploring Affect in the Postfeminist, Visual Moral Economy of *My Big Fat Gypsy Wedding*," *Feminst Media Studies* 14.3 (2014): 370.

27. Stephens, 171.

28. Mormonism is its own faith with its own doctrine and scriptures, and not a denomination of Protestant Christianity. The mainstream LDS Church would no doubt be extremely resistant to being understood as just another Protestant denomination. However, the Christian Bible is one of its holy books, even if not its primary scripture. Because the Browns are not part of the mainstream LDS Church and because they tend to discuss their faith in the language of lifestyling, I argue that their family does fit this brand pattern.

29. Tanya D. Zuk, "'Proud Mormon Polygamist': Assimilation, Popular Memory, and the Mormon Churches in *Big Love*," *Journal of Religion and Popular Culture* 26.1 (Spring 2014): 101.

30. Its episodic programs, in which viewers identify less with character and more with the process of excessive consumption, are more racially diverse. The wedding block frequently features women of color although they are still a clear representational minority. *Say Yes to the Dress* (2007–), *Say Yes to the Dress Atlanta* (2010–), and *A Wedding Story* (1996–) are examples of these episodic programs.

31. Programs like *Little People, Big World* (2006–) and *The Little Couple* (2009–), for example, follow families with different types of dwarfism as they work, raise children, struggle with health issues, and in the case of *Little Couple*, adopt children. Jennifer Arnold, one half of the titular *Little Couple*, is a physician and Matthew Roloff, the father of the *Little People, Big World* family, has an array of chronic health issues both related and un-related to his dwarfism. Because of these characters, both shows spend a considerable amount of time in hospitals and doctors' offices and these settings offer a context for performers to straightforwardly discuss living with dwarfism and the repercussions it can have on one's health. One could argue that these moments medicalize the experience of disability and distance it from any lived experience; in fact, the focus on relationships inherent to this style of reality television ensures that both discourses coexist. The pursuit of having children or the constant reconstitution of the nuclear family after trauma or argument overwhelm any othering that takes place and recuperates these families into dominant norms of whiteness.

32. Banet-Weiser, 169.
33. Pierre Bourdieu, *Distinction: A Social Critique of the Judgment of Taste*, trans. Richard Nice, (Boston: Harvard University Press, 1984).
34. Madeleine Schwartz, "The Polygamists Come Out," *Dissent* 61.3 (Summer 2014): 11.
35. Laura Harrison and Sarah B. Rowley, "Babies by the Bundle: Gender, Backlash, and the Quiverfull movement," *Feminist Formations* 23.1 (Spring 2011): 53.
36. Sarah Palin, during her Vice Presidential candidacy in 2008, distinguished between "real America," the conservative, religious, "red state," blue-collar workers who lived in suburbs and small towns, and the urban, supposedly wealthier, more educated, secular "blue state" coastal liberals.
37. Laurie Ouellette, "Branding the Right: The Affective Economy of Sarah Palin," *Cinema Journal* 51.4 (Summer 2012): 185–91.
38. Christopher Lockett, "Masculinity and Authenticity: Reality TV's Real Men," Flowtv.org 13.01 (October 5, 2010).
39. Victoria E. Johnson, *Heartland TV: Prime Time Television and the Struggle for U.S. Identity*, (New York: New York University Press, 2008), 5.
40. Fiona Duncan, "Normcore: Fashion for Those Who Realize They're One in 7 billion," *New York Magazine* February 26, 2014.
41. "*19 Kids and Counting* Son Named in Underage Sex Probe," *In Touch Weekly* May 19, 2015. Available online at www.intouchweekly.com/posts/19-kids-and-counting-son-named-in-underage-sex-probe-58751 (accessed February 12, 2016).
42. "Improper touching" is the phrase Michelle and Jim Bob Duggar used to describe Josh's behavior in an interview with journalist Megyn Kelly. "Michelle and Jim Bob Duggar: Sisters 'Weren't Even Aware' of Josh's 'Wrongdoing,'" FoxNews.com June 4, 2015. Available online at www.foxnews.com/entertainment/2015/06/03/were-devastated-michelle-duggar-tells-megyn-kelly-about-son-actions/ (accessed February 12, 2016).
43. "Josh Duggar Chilling Molestation Confession in New Police Report," *In Touch Weekly.com*, June 3, 2015. Available online at www.intouchweekly.com/posts/josh-duggar-chilling-molestation-confession-in-new-police-report-59752 (accessed February 12, 2016).

5 Looking Forward
Cracks in the Foundation of Postfeminism and Mommy Culture

Early twenty-first century popular culture is indisputably in the throes of postfeminist mommy culture. I began this book describing the ultimate contemporary mom. She is well-off, slender, suburban- or urban-dwelling, in her 30s or 40s, usually white, and utterly devoted to her children. Indeed, her children and her maternal status are the primary locus of her identity and the indicators that she is a complete adult woman. That picture of the heroic, self-sacrificing mother functions to create an image of the most culturally and economically valued modes of womanhood, and citizenship more generally, in the early twenty-first century. Like historical versions of this maternal ideal from the Victorian Angel in the House to the mid-twentieth century Happy Homemaker, twenty-first century hypernatalism is spurred on by a confluence of social, economic, and political crises. In the face of a dire recession, surges in legal and illegal immigration, shifting definitions of marriage to be more inclusive, and popular protest movements coalescing around income inequality and police violence against African Americans, images of white middle- and upper-class mothers form a cultural bulwark against traumatic change. Mommy culture is one visible manifestation of the ways in which women's reproductive bodies are mobilized as a political battleground for unspoken or unspeakable ideological clashes about the future of the nation and what kinds of people are the most culturally valued citizens. In this era, those people are affluent, entrepreneurial subjects who have internalized neoliberal emphases on the individual or the family as isolated economic and social units. For women, the "correct" path toward that achievement is via self-branding, turning the affective labor of relationship maintenance into the remunerative labor of selling consumer goods. One of the most effective routes toward self-branding, this book has argued, is via motherhood and the softening of potentially feminist achievement by articulating it in terms of postfeminist valorization of maternity. "New momism," as Susan Douglas and Meredith Michaels have labeled it, or the "new domesticity," in Emily Matchar's words, enshrines women within the domestic roles of wife and mother and frames those private unpaid positions as a nostalgic return to forgotten modes of empowerment rather than an evacuation of women out of public life.[1]

Confronted with crises like recession, and social and political conflicts around racial inequality, immigration, and new definitions of marriage and family, the heroic maternal is asked to bear the ideological burden of representing the unspeakable or embodying irreconcilable cultural tensions. In the real world, this takes the form of ever-harsher legal limits on women's access to reproductive choice and health care more generally. US states continue to enforce mandatory maternity by preventing access to contraception and abortion. Republican presidential candidates in 2016 promised to defund Planned Parenthood, an affordable women's healthcare provider with semi-publicly funded offices throughout the US, and Louisiana became the most recent state to reduce the number of abortion providers to one.[2] Within popular culture, the overdetermined meaning of motherhood is evidenced by the proliferation of images of mothers and the relative absence of women with identities defined as outside the maternal or pre-maternal.

Because twenty-first century popular culture also overvalues fame, I've argued that celebrity women's maternal bodies serve as instruction manuals of a sort for proper postfeminist citizenship. Since authenticity and ordinariness are the most valued modes of contemporary stardom, reality personalities and celebrities promoting self-brands, rather than characters or movie star personae, bear the heaviest part of that representational burden. Their connection to "the real" via self-performance is tight enough that they are understood to be presenting a form of reality. Even the most sophisticated audiences, skilled in reading brand construction and performances of authenticity as marketing endeavors, cannot disavow that they are seeing real people conceive and parent their actual children onscreen. That realness, no matter how performed, adds ideological heft to those representations, hence, my focus here on reality TV and associated forms of celebrity. As they create self-brands and perform motherhood, these celebrities and their children formulate a picture of the ways women should cope with recession and inequality, i.e. by returning to the domestic sphere, refashioning affective and domestic labor into entrepreneurialism, and maintaining a slender, youthful, contained body ideal. As we have observed, the most lasting and lucrative of those celebrity personalities are those who are best able to centralize motherhood in a brand identity that crosses platforms from television to tabloid culture, and from the Internet to bricks and mortar retail stores. The celebrity and reality performances of the likes of Kate Middleton, Kim Kardashian, Giuliana Rancic, and Jessica Alba, along with their children, work to shore up images of future nations free from the social issues that instigate hypernatalist popular culture. Middleton and her royal family envisage a sunny, white UK free from class distinctions; Kardashian, Rancic, and Alba imagine a postracial America in which the hetero-family as a powerhouse economic unit alleviates the need for social reform or financial regulation.

These deeply dissatisfying ideals are extraordinarily limiting even for the affluent white women they address, and they are unreachable by poor women and women of color who are disproportionately victimized by policies such as the continued removal of access to women's health care, a lack of parental leave in the United States, and low-paying jobs that inadequately cover the costs of childcare they require. Even within the images of perfect entrepreneurial motherhood, fault lines begin to appear. Gwyneth Paltrow's refusal to place her children and her motherhood at the center of her GOOP lifestyle brand, I have argued, is part of what taints her image with out-of-touch elitism. When Kardashian, for another example, publicly discusses how uncomfortable and ill she was throughout her first pregnancy and how difficult it was to conceive a second child, she disrupts the picture of silently suffering, sacrificial motherhood. Similarly, Rancic's attempts to conceive were thwarted by her professional requirement as an entertainment news presenter to stay extremely slender in order to wear high fashion even before she was diagnosed with breast cancer that prevented her pregnancy. These women's difficult pregnancies depicted them as more heroic and sacrificing mothers when they finally did have kids. Not everyone, however, even reality personalities and celebrities, are able to live up to the demands of postfeminist mommy culture. In the face of these dissatisfactions and injustices, various feminisms are beginning to emerge. In this final epilogue, I examine ways the postfeminist maternal ideal is being made visible via failure to live up to its parameters. I continue to briefly explore celebrity feminism, particularly its presence in Hillary Clinton's presidential campaign, and its limitations before arguing that postfeminist mommy culture as well as the limits of affluent white feminism are in fact being challenged, and perhaps creating potential for more inclusive emerging feminisms.

Postfeminist Failure: Cracks in the Foundation

Instances of postfeminist failure have cropped up throughout this book—failure to live up to the early twenty-first century postfeminist ideals of body, age, race, class, authenticity, relatability, or fertility and the standards of postfeminist mommy culture. Bravo's brand identity, as discussed in Chapter Two, actually celebrates the unruliness and the failures of its best loved stars to understand and adhere to the impossibly contradictory demands of intensive motherhood, self-branding, and hyperfemininity. The playfulness with which Bravo frames those failures and the popularity of visibly, continually unruly performers like Ramona Singer and NeNe Leakes position Bravo as a haven for discontent with motherhood-obsessed postfeminism. In the same vein, Jessica Alba's public relations feud with Gwyneth Paltrow leads to the frustrating conclusion that feminized popular culture only has space on top for one version of perfect mother-centric lifestyling at a time. Finally, the Duggar family brand disintegrated when Michelle Duggar's narrative and brand centricity along with the wholesome picture of an "average," if enormous, rural family were revealed to be nothing more than well-branded performances. These images of failure, feuding, and inability on the part of even the elite to live up to the demands of contemporary postfeminist mommy culture reveals, I hope, the shaky foundations of that ideology.

Blake Lively's lifestyle venture, Preserve, which folded in October 2015 after just over a year online, serves as an example of the ways in which such a failure can offer cultural potential. In many ways, Preserve repeated the retreatist family narrative and Southern regional identity of Reese Witherspoon's Draper James (see Chapter Three). Preserve was found online at Preserve.us, an address that evokes the phrase "preserve us," a quaint, vaguely Southern saying in keeping with the site's gauzy nostalgic aesthetic. The web address also hints at the fact that all products available through the site are made in the United States by small businesses the site always labeled artisans. Each business partner had a blurb on the site explaining either their origin story or their ethical perspective on production. Just like the claims to localism and small batch or ethical production on the successful sites run by Witherspoon, Jessica Alba, and Monica Potter, all Preserve's partners claim some combination of local, repurposed, organic, natural, or artisanal manufacture. Lively was even savvy enough to announce her first pregnancy on the site. The announcement, which also served to advertise the shirt covering her pregnant belly, was a clear effort to rebrand her persona in contrast to her best known acting role as louche socialite Serena van der Woodsen on the teen soap *Gossip Girl* (CW 2007–12). The image, which was a medium close-up that showed Lively from lips to hips, but removed any agency or identification by cutting off her eyes and the top of her head, featured earth tones and a rural setting, completing her transformation from New York City-based wild child on *Gossip Girl* to demure Southern mother and lifestyle guide. Yet the site began its rapid demise with an October 2014 advertorial called "The Allure of Antebellum."[3] Ostensibly a celebration of the same Southern charm working so well for Witherspoon, this spread, featuring all white models (although models of color were visible if a user scrolled or clicked through to actually purchase items described in the photo story), harkened specifically to a pre-Civil War past. "The term 'Southern Belle,'" the story read, "came to fruition during the Antebellum period (prior to the Civil War), acknowledging women with an inherent social distinction who set the standards for style and appearance." The direct reference to slave-owning Southerners as women with an inborn class distinction manages to articulate the most racist discourses of "natural" or biological racial difference of the nineteenth century in an attempt to sell clothing to white women. Gawker reported on the story under the headline "Blake Lively's Fall Fashion Inspiration is Slaveowners," and received a cease and desist letter from Lively's attorney alleging Gawker was illegally defaming Lively.[4] This horrid public relations event eventually spelled the demise of the brand. Preserve's catastrophic failure, however, like the feuds and foibles described above, disrupts the smooth surface of the dominant ideology. By basing the brand on a white identity that seemed willing (albeit presumably unconsciously) to admit the violent oppressive history that supported that nostalgic ideal, Preserve's failure destabilized whiteness and the power of white celebrity pregnancy and motherhood to cover over contemporary inequalities. Thus, failure to successfully execute the move from television star to maternal lifestyle brand calls attention to precisely the conflicts the fetishized image of maternity is meant to cover over. Taken together, all of these failures might even suggest a subtle refusal to continue participating in these neoliberal logics and a hope for alternative representations of motherhood, increased intersectionality, and full female subjectivity.

After Postfeminism, Emerging Feminisms

While feuding and failing work to expose the cracks in the dominant ideals and reveal the ideologies they support, avowedly feminist voices are still sparse. For example, Reese Witherspoon's voice, as discussed in Chapter Three, is present in the rhetoric she uses to promote her film production company but is typically hidden in her lifestyle brand. Other white celebrities like actresses Lena Dunham and Amy Poehler have made feminism part of their public personae; Dunham, in particular, has been criticized for the privileged, highly educated, white version of young womanhood and potential feminism she represents on her TV dramedy *Girls* (HBO 2012–2017). Indeed, celebrity feminism by definition brings with it the privilege of wealth and fame, and like the Hollywood from which it draws, often assumes a white norm. Most of these white celebrity feminists—we could add Geena Davis, Susan Sarandon, Tina Fey, and Emma Watson to the list—intriguingly do not discuss motherhood (although most of them are mothers). Unlike the women throughout this book, they do not use motherhood to support their brands or personae, nor does motherhood appear as a central site of identity formation for them as it does for women capitalizing on new momism. While I welcome a move away from motherhood as the only acceptable mode of identity formation for women, its relative absence from these women's overtly feminist brands implies an incompatibility between feminism and motherhood that shows signs, perhaps, of excluding poorer women who have less access to contraception or childcare and, therefore, may be less able to forge a public identity separate from child rearing.

Scholars, popular culture figures, and politicians alike have begun to grapple in recent years with understanding and defining the evident shift away from the postfeminist norms of hyperfeminine displays of fashion, excessive consumption, and focus on heterosexual romance, marriage, and family as the central features of female identity. Diane Negra and Yvonne Tasker note that "the cultures of the recession are giving license to new expressions of female anger and resentment in a trend that evokes the early 1990s films of an earlier recession like *Thelma and Louise* (1991) and *Basic Instinct* (1992)."[5] The most cited version of this to come out of the 2007–08 recession is likely *Girls*, which Meredith Nash and Ruby Grant suggest illustrates a transitional next wave of "post?femininsm."[6] Anne Helen Petersen helpfully describes this early twenty-first century batch of unruly young women—notably putting off marriage and motherhood—as visualizing a "postfeminist dystopia" that sets stories like the romantic comedies *Trainwreck* (2015) and *The Mindy Project* (Fox 2012–15; Hulu 2015–) within the cultural milieu of postfeminism but expresses deep dissatisfaction with the extremely limited options it offers women for full adult subjectivity.[7]

In 2016, the US is also in the midst of a presidential election featuring Hillary Clinton, the first genuinely viable female candidate (although she is genuinely viable for the second time; the first being against Barack Obama in 2008) essentially necessitating a public reengagement with female achievement and feminist rhetoric. Clinton's fellow front-runners during the primary election cycle were Donald Trump, who consistently spouted reactionary, racist, misogynist, and anti-intellectual vitriol, and self-avowed Democratic Socialist Bernie Sanders on the left. Such a stark divide between right and left, exacerbated by Trump's blustery oratory, made contemporary inequalities central features of the lengthy campaign cycle. In response, Clinton recruited a multi-racial, multi-generational collective of celebrity women to endorse her in explicitly gendered terms.

As the first female front-runner candidate, feminism, female collectivity, and precisely which demographics of women voters supported her were prominent, consistent parts of Clinton's media coverage. Female celebrities ranging in age from their 20s to their 60s, women like Shonda Rhimes, Lena Dunham, Amy Poehler, Uzo Aduba, Gina Rodriguez, and Jamie Lee Curtis, publicly supported Clinton's campaign. They posed for photos, posted Hillary's campaign messages on social media, and contributed to widely reported campaign videos explaining why "I'm with her."[8] Yet polling indicated that young women, so-called millennials, favored Bernie Sanders, a 74-year-old white man, by a wide margin in the primary elections.[9] Those young women were, in turn, criticized by older feminist icons from Gloria Steinem to former Secretary of State Madeleine Albright, who said at a Clinton rally that "There's a special place in hell for women who don't help each other."[10] This lack of gender solidarity was framed in the press as a generational conflict that demonstrated younger voters' distrust of Clinton's establishment credentials (despite Sanders's twenty-five years in Congress). Alongside the rhetoric of Clinton's supposed failure to appeal to young women, an idea circulated of unmarried women, with and without children, as a growing demographic with sudden power to sway politics.[11]

Pollsters and prognosticators noted the power of unmarried women voters pushing candidates to address issues like parental leave, better access to all forms of health care, equal pay, and higher minimum wages.[12] Journalist Rebecca Traister went so far as to argue that the sharp rise in the number of single women in the electorate was actually creating "an entirely new category of citizen."[13] Feminism is still a word uttered only cautiously in political circles, but the prominence of discourse about women (married or unmarried), their relationship to and demands on the public State, represents a cultural shift from a postfeminist understanding of women solely as private consumers, mothers, and potential mothers. As I finish writing in the Spring of 2016, economic recovery from the recession is ongoing. As the restrictions on women's reproductive rights and the intensity of the post-feminist demands of body and brand control have become too visibly rigid and frustrating, we begin to see a renewed need for organized feminism. The stricter the limits, the more women see the cracks in the dominant ideology and begin to work to expand those cracks by claiming the term feminist.

A Way Forward with Beyoncé

On February 6, 2016, the day before the Super Bowl at which she performed, Beyoncé released a music video for her song "Formation." The song and video launched a thousand think pieces about the singer's mobilization of pop culture and her (massive) celebrity for activist goals, but definitively answered questions about the legitimacy of her feminism in the affirmative.[14] A couple of years earlier, during her performance at the 2014 Video Music Awards (VMAs), Beyoncé stopped, center stage, silhouetted in front of a giant screen with the word feminist emblazoned across it, igniting the initial conversation about whether her feminism "counted" when coupled wither her fame and the commercialism of the setting. Nathalie Weidhase demonstrates how criticisms of Beyoncé's identification as a feminist were often rooted in her celebrity, her blackness, and the sexuality of her dance performance.[15] Racialized critiques of her right to call herself a feminist were masked in generational conflicts, but also in her celebration of her own marriage and motherhood evidenced by her choosing the title Mrs. Carter for her 2013–14 world tour, and being presented her Lifetime Achievement Award at those 2014 VMAs by her husband and daughter.

Beyoncé's negotiation of political feminism within postfeminist celebrity and motherhood continues in "Formation." The presence of children, her own and others, in her performances and music videos illustrates the representational power of children but also demonstrates motherhood as another site in which she negotiates her identities against contemporary dominant norms and ideals. Dayna Chatman has argued that Beyoncé hails "women as self-governing subjects who make the right choices with respect to career, marriage, motherhood, and the disciplining of their bodies."[16] Yet more than repeating the same disciplinary functions postfeminism places on the idealized white mother, Beyoncé's claim to the title feminist acknowledges the constraints of postfeminist entrepreneurial motherhood and begins to reject them. Because she is Beyoncé, perhaps the most famous woman in the world, and certainly a widely adored musician and pop culture figure, her hypervisible challenges to the white, retreatist, child-obsessed, maternal ideal carry enormous potential.

Among the many powerful images of Southern blackness in the "Formation" video, two images of children stand out for this analysis. The children in "Formation" serve the same function as the children discussed in

Chapter One to point toward ideas of a future nation. However, where Kate Middleton and Kim Kardashian's children embody a future free from class and race conflicts, in "Formation," the images of children are contemporary and overtly political. A young boy in a hoody sweatshirt dances in front of a line of police in riot gear before stopping, arms out-stretched, in front of the officers who raise their hands in a don't shoot gesture just before the video cuts to graffiti reading "stop shooting us." This child envisions not the adorable postracial future embodied by Kim Kardashian and Kanye West's daughter North but asks directly for a respite from racialized police violence. Beyoncé references her own maternity as well by including a scene of her daughter Blue Ivy. The inclusion of Blue Ivy among a series of images of black women, and never in the same frame as her mother, positions her more as representative of a future generation. Indeed, the four-year-old is given her own agency and identity, centralized in the frame, hands on hips, looking directly into the camera. The video does not confine children's identity to cuteness, and it displays Beyoncé's motherhood as part of, but not constitutive of, her identity. Thus, Beyoncé's maternity and her daughter's image are part of the singer's political statement about diverse black femininity and, indeed, black personhood in the face of continued representational and literal racial violence in the United States. Motherhood is put in service of identity, but an overtly political identity rather than a commoditized self-branding opportunity. One pop singer and one music video, no matter how rich the popular response, does not indicate a sea change from postfeminism to feminism, from motherhood as the only valid path to female adulthood to just one among many possibilities. Yet the strength of this one voice and its position outside of and in contention with dominant white postfeminist mother-centric identities offer a real challenge to that dominant ideal and hint at a wider cultural shift toward feminism, intersectionality, and motherhood as only one element of a complex female adulthood.

This book has focused on so-called quality texts and their affluent stars and affluent or aspirational target audiences. The quality texts, affluent performers, and audiences they target are all symbols of economic boom and its desired return, as well as sometimes scapegoats for the massive frustrations of income inequality and a growing recognition that the aspirational, entrepreneurial, branded self is impossible for most women, and perhaps even undesirable. That focus on the wealthy has functioned as a way to fully understand the most culturally and economically valued forms of celebrity, branding, and maternity. Abject or "bad" mothers can shore up an ideal by contrast, so what happens when women who fit the supposed ideal themselves compete with each other, acknowledge how hard they work, how much (paid) support they receive, and still sometimes fail to meet the standards of perfect postfeminist motherhood? Rather than failures, these moments can be understood as ruptures in the dominant ideology. They are cracks that display the impossible constraints and help reveal unspoken racist and classist ideologies behind images of perfection. By collecting images of failure, unruliness, not-quite-success, or even simple exhaustion, we can begin to assemble a case against postfeminism and a picture of the kinds of feminism produced by intense dissatisfaction with postfeminism. Ideology works because it is invisible. Failure to adhere to norms or achieve ideals by the very people meant to embody those ideals makes ideology visible. That visibility is the beginning of challenge, and while the hypervalorization of middle- and upper-class white motherhood is not yet under threat, the extraordinary difficulty of attaining the ideal is more readable in these popular cultural failures. While the most recognizable emerging feminisms are rightfully criticized as too white, too invested in celebrity, and too elitist, they can and do challenge the dominant norms of postfeminism, including the heroic maternal, retreatism, and the self and family as the primary locus of emotional and paid labor. Perhaps a truly collective, intersectional feminism has yet to emerge but the failures and the successes of celebrity mothers like Beyoncé, who work and succeed outside that mold, point toward imminent potential.

Notes

1. Susan Douglas and Meredith Michaels, "Introduction," *The Mommy Myth: The Idealization of Motherhood and How It Has Undermined All Women* (New York: Free Press, 2004), Kindle Edition; Emily Matchar, *Homeward Bound: Why Women Are Embracing the New Domesticity*, (New York: Simon & Schuster, 2013), Kindle Edition.
2. Becca Andrews, "This Court Ruling Brings Another State Down to One Abortion Clinic," *Mother Jones* February 24, 2016.
3. "Allure of Antebellum," Preserve.us October 2014 (accessed November 2, 2014).
4. Allie Jones, "Blake Lively's Fall Fashion Inspiration Is Slaveowners," *Gawker* October 13, 2014. Available online at http://gawker.com/blake-livelys-fall-fashion-inspiration-is-slaveowners-1645661587 (accessed December 11, 2014); Max Read, "Blake Lively's Lawyer Wants Us to Take Down This Post," *Gawker* October 14, 2014. Available online at http://gawker.com/blake-livelys-fall-fashion-inspiration-is-slaveowners-1645661587/1646150135/+maxread (accessed December 11, 2014).
5. Diane Negra and Yvonne Tasker, "Introduction: Gender and Recessionary Culture," *Gendering the Recession: Media and Culture in an Age of Austerity*, Negra and Tasker, eds. (Durham, NC: Duke University Press, 2014), 18.
6. Meredith Nash and Ruby Grant, "Twenty-Something *Girls* vs. Thirty-Something *Sex and the City* Women: Paving the Way for Post?Feminism," *Feminist Media Studies* 15.6 (2015): 976–91.
7. Anne Helen Petersen, "In *Trainwreck*, Amy Schumer Calls Bullshit on Postfeminism," Buzzfeed July 18, 2015. Available online at www.buzzfeed.com/annehelenpetersen/postfeminist-bullshit#.qcDboNRMN (accessed February 27, 2016).
8. Shonda Rhimes is the creator and producer of *Grey's Anatomy* (ABC 2005–) and *Scandal* (ABC 2012–); Lena Dunham is the creator, writer, and star of *Girls*; Amy Poehler is best known for sitcom *Parks and Recreation* (NBC 2009–15);

Uzo Aduba is an Emmy-award winning actress for *Orange Is the New Black* (Netflix 2013–); and Gina Rodriguez is the Golden Globe winning star of *Jane the Virgin* (CW 2014–). All of these women appear, among other places, in a campaign video publicized with the hashtag #ImWithHer. See, for example, Chris Serico, "#ImWithHer: Jamie Lee Curtis, Shonda Rhimes among Clebs Backing Hillary Clinton," *Today* February 1, 2016. Available online at www.today.com/popculture/imwithher-jamie-lee-curtis-shonda-rhimes-among-celebs-backing-hillary-t70521 (accessed February 23, 2016).

9. See, for example, Ronald Brownstein, "The Great Democratic Age Gap," *The Atlantic* February 2, 2016. Available online at www.theatlantic.com/politics/archive/2016/02/the-great-democratic-age-gap/459570/ (accessed February 23, 2016); Brian Hanley, "Young Women Prefer Sanders to Clinton and It Has Nothing to Do with Impressing the Boys," *Huffington Post* February 7, 2016. Available online at www.huffingtonpost.com/brian-hanley/young-women-prefer-sander_b_9182756.html (accessed February 23, 2016); Elizabeth Breunig, "Why Are Millennial Women Gravitating to Bernie Sanders?" *The New Republic* February 9, 2016. Available online at https://newrepublic.com/article/129483/millennial-women-gravitating-bernie-sanders (accessed February 23, 2016).

10. The comment was made when Albright introduced Clinton at a rally before the New Hampshire primary. Tom McCarthy, "Albright: 'Special Place in Hell' for Women Who Don't Support Clinton," *The Guardian* February 6, 2016. Available online at www.theguardian.com/us-news/2016/feb/06/madeleine-albright-campaigns-for-hillary-clinton (accessed February 23, 2016).

11. Rebecca Traister, "The Single American Woman," *New York* February 22, 2016. The article was adapted from her forthcoming book, *All the Single Ladies: Unmarried Women and the Rise of an Independent Nation* (New York: Simon & Schuster, 2016).

12. Marc Ambinder, "Five Things You Need to Know Before Predicting the 2016 Election," FiveThirtyEight.com September 15, 2015 (accessed February 25, 2016); Jessica Valenti, "Single Ladies Have Increasing Impact in a Culture that Still Dismisses Them," *The Guardian* February 24, 2016.

13. Traister, "The Single American Woman."

14. See, for example, Syreeta McFadden, "Beyoncé's Formation Reclaims Black America's Narrative from the Margins," *The Guardian* February 8, 2016; Jessica Williams, "Beyoncé's Halftime Show Message," *The Daily Show* February 8, 2016. Available online at www.cc.com/video-clips/j79s76/the-daily-show-with-trevor-noah-beyonce-s-halftime-show-message (accessed February 25, 2016); Danielle C. Belton, "Beyoncé Drops 'Formation' for the People, the Black People," *The Root* February 7, 2016. Available online at www.theroot.com/articles/culture/2016/02/beyonce_drops_formation_for_the_people_the_black_people.html (accessed February 25, 2016).

15. Nathalie Weidhase summarizes the criticisms of Beyoncé's feminism, and using pop singer Annie Lennox's critique as exemplary, illustrates their bases in racially and generationally exclusionary understandings of feminism. Nathalie Weidhase, "'Beyoncé Feminism' and the Contestation of the Black Feminist Body," *Celebrity Studies* 6.1 (online January 2015): 128–31.

16. Dayna Chatman, "Pregnancy, Then It's 'Back to Business:' Beyoncé, Black Femininity, and the Politics of a Post-Feminist Gender Regime," *Feminist Media Studies* 15.6 (2015): 926–41.

Bibliography

Affuso, Elizabeth. "'Don't Just Watch It—Live It:' Technology, Corporate Partnership, and *The Hills.*" *Jump Cut* 51 (Spring 2009).

Banet-Weiser, Sarah. *Authentic™: The Politics of Ambivalence in a Brand Culture* (New York: New York University Press, 2012).

Becker, Ron. "'Help is on the Way!': *Supernanny, Nanny 911* and the Neoliberal Politics of the Family." *The Great American Makeover: Television, History, Nation,* Dana Heller, ed. (New York: Palgrave-Macmillan, 2006).

Beltrán, Mary C. "The Hollywood Latina Body as Site of Social Struggle: Media Constructions of Stardom and Jennifer Lopez's 'Cross-Over Butt.'" *Quarterly Review of Film & Video* 19 (2002): 71–86.

Mary Beltrán. *Latina/o Stars in U.S. Eyes: The Making and Meanings of Film and TV Stardom* (Urbana and Chicago: University of Illinois Press, 2009).

Bennett, James. "The Television Personality System: Televisual Stardom Revisited after Film Theory." *Screen* 49.1 (Spring 2008): 32–50.

Berlant, Lauren. "America, 'Fat,' the Fetus." *boundary 2* 21.3 (Autumn 1994): 145–95.

Bevan, Alex. "The National Body, Women, and Mental Health in *Homeland.*" *Analyzing Homeland*, Diane Negra and Jorie Lagerwey, eds. *Cinema Journal In Focus* 54.4 (August 2015).

Bourdieu, Pierre. *Distinction: A Social Critique of the Judgment of Taste*, trans. Richard Nice (Boston: Harvard University Press, 1984).

Brunsdon, Charlotte. "Problems with Quality." *Screen* 31, no. 1 (1990): 67–90.

Cobb, Shelley. "Mother of the Year: Kathy Hilton, Lynne Spears, Dina Lohan, and Bad Celebrity Motherhood." *Genders* 48 (2008). Online journal.

Cusk, Rachel. *A Life's Work: On Becoming a Mother* (London: Fourth Estate, 2001).

Chatman, Dayna. "Pregnancy, Then It's 'Back to Business:' Beyoncé, Black Femininity, and the Politics of a Post-Feminist Gender Regime." *Feminist Media Studies* 15.6 (2015): 926–41.

Dominguez, Pier. "'I'm Very Rich, Bitch!': The Melodramatic Money Shot and the Excess of Racialized Gendered Affect in the *Real Housewives* Docusoaps." *Camera Obscura* 88, 30.1 (2015): 155–83.

Dyer, Richard. *Stars* (London: BFI Press, 1979).

Dyer, Richard. *White* (London: Routledge, 1997).

Feuer, Jane. "'Quality' Reality and the Bravo Media Reality Series." *Camera Obscura* 30.1 (2015): 185–95.

Feuer, Jane, Paul Kerr, and Tise Vahimagi, eds. *MTM: Quality Television* (London: BFI, 1984).

Gates, Racquel. "Activating the Negative Image." *Television and New Media* 16.7 (2015): 616–30.

Gill, Rosalind. "Postfeminist Media Culture: Elements of a Sensibility." *European Journal of Cultural Studies* 10.2 (2007): 147–66.

Hall, Stuart. "Encoding, Decoding." *The Cultural Studies Reader*, Simon During, ed. (London: Routledge, 1993), 90–103.

Hanson, Clare. *A Cultural History of Pregnancy: Pregnancy, Medicine and Culture, 1750–2000* (New York: Palgrave-MacMillan, 2004).

Harrison, Laura and Sarah B. Rowley. "Babies by the Bundle: Gender, Backlash, and the Quiverfull Movement." *Feminist Formations* 23.1 (Spring 2011): 47–69.

Hearn, Allison. "'Meat, Mask, Burden:' Probing the Contours of the Branded 'Self.'" *Journal of Consumer Culture* 8.2 (2008): 197–217.

Jensen, Tracey and Jessica Ringrose. "Sluts that Choose vs. Doormat Gypsies: Exploring Affect in the Postfeminist, Visual Moral Economy of *My Big Fat Gypsy Wedding*." *Feminist Media Studies* 14.3 (2014): 369–87.

Johnson, Victoria E. *Heartland TV: Prime Time Television and the Struggle for U.S. Identity* (New York: New York University Press, 2008).

Jones, Jennifer Lynn and Brenda R. Weber. "Reality Moms, Real Monsters: Transmediated Continuity, Reality Celebrity, and the Female Grotesque." *Camera Obscura* 30.1 (2015): 11–39.

Keller, Jessalynn Marie. "Fiercely Real?: Tyra Banks and the Making of New Media Celebrity." *Feminist Media Studies* (2012), Online First Edition. Available online at http://dx.doi.org/10.1080/14680777.2012.740490 (accessed September 20, 2013).

Klein, Amanda Ann. "Welfare Queen Redux: *Teen Mom*, Class and the Bad Mother." *Flow* 13.03 (November 12, 2010).

Kukla, Rebecca. *Mass Hysteria: Medicine, Culture, and Mothers' Bodies* (Lanham, Maryland: Rowman & Littlefield Publishers, 2005).

Levine, Elana, ed. *Cupcakes, Pinterest, and Ladyporn: Feminized Popular Culture in the Early Twenty-First Century* (Urbana-Champaign: University of Illinois Press, 2015).

Littler, Jo. "The Rise of the 'Yummy Mummy:' Popular Conservatism and the Neoliberal Maternal in Contemporary British Culture." *Communication, Culture & Critique* 6 (2013): 227–43.

Lockett, Christopher. "Masculinity and Authenticity: Reality TV's Real Men." Flowtv.org 13.01 (October 5, 2010).

Lopez, Lori Kido. "The Radical Act of 'Mommy Blogging:' Redefining Motherhood Through the Blogosphere." *New Media & Society* 11.5 (2009): 729–47.

Marwick, Alice and danah boyd. "To See and Be Seen: Celebrity Practice on Twitter." *Convergence* 17.2 (May 2011): 139–58.

Matchar, Emily. *Homeward Bound: Why Women Are Embracing the New Domesticity* (New York: Simon & Schuster, 2013), Kindle Edition.

McIntyre, Anthony. "Isn't She Adorkable!: Cuteness as Political Neutralization in the Star Text of Zooey Deschanel." *Television and New Media*, Online First Edition, Feb 28, 2014, doi: 10.1177/1527476414524284.

McRobbie, Angela. "Post-feminism and Popular Culture." *Media Studies: A Reader*, 3rd ed., eds. Sue Thornham, Caroline Bassett, and Paul Marris (New York: New York University Press, 2009).

Meyers, Erin. "Gossip Blogs and 'Baby Bumps': The New Visual Spectacle of Female Celebrity in Gossip Media." *The Handbook of Gender, Sex, & Media*, Karen Ross, ed. (Oxford: Wiley-Blackwell Press, 2012), 53–70.

Modeleski, Tania. "The Search for Tomorrow in Today's Soap Opera." *Feminist Television Criticism*, eds. Charlotte Brunsdon, Julie D'Acci, and Lynn Spigel (Oxford: Oxford University Press, 1997), 36–47.

Morrison, Aimée. "'Suffused by Feeling and Affect:' The Intimate Public of Personal Mommy Blogging." *Biography* 34.1 (Winter 2011): 37–55.

Mukherjee, Roopali and Sarah Banet-Weiser, eds. *Commodity Activism: Cultural Resistance in Neoliberal Times* (New York: New York University, 2012).

Murray, Susan and Laurie Ouellette, eds. *Reality TV: Remaking Television Culture*, 2nd ed. (New York: New York University Press, 2009).

Nash, Meredith and Ruby Grant. "Twenty-Something *Girls* vs. Thirty-Something *Sex and the City* Women: Paving the Way for Post?feminism." *Feminist Media Studies* 15.6 (2015): 976–91.

Negra, Diane. *Off-White Hollywood: American Culture and Ethnic Female Stardom* (New York: Routledge, 2001).

Negra, Diane. *What a Girl Wants?: Fantasizing the Reclamation of the Self in Post-feminism* (London & New York: Routledge, 2009).

Newman, Michael Z. and Elana Levine. *Legitimating Television* (New York: Routeldge, 2011).

Oliver, Kelly. *Knock Me Up, Knock Me Down: Images of Pregnancy in Hollywood Films* (New York: Columbia University Press, 2012).

Ouellette, Laurie. "Branding the Right: The Affective Economy of Sarah Palin." *Cinema Journal* 51.4 (Summer 2012): 185–91.

Ouellette, Laurie and James Hay. *Better Living Through Reality Television: Television and Post-Welfare Citizenship* (Malden, MA: Blackwell Publishing, 2008).

Petersen, Anne Helen. "In *Trainwreck*, Amy Schumer Calls Bullshit on Postfeminism," Buzzfeed July 18, 2015. Available online at www.buzzfeed.com/annehelenpetersen/postfeminist-bullshit#.qcDboNRMN (accessed February 27, 2016).

Plant, Rebecca Jo. *Mom: The Transformation of Motherhood in Modern America* (Chicago: University of Chicago Press, 2010).

Ryan, Maureen. "Feminist Housewife Blogger." Paper presented at the Society for Cinema and Media Studies Conference (Boston, MA, March 21–25, 2012).

Sandberg, Sheryl. *Lean In: Women, Work, and the Will to Lead* (New York: Knopf, 2013).

Schwartz, Madeleine. "The Polygamists Come Out." *Dissent* 61.3 (Summer 2014).

Sender, Katherine. "Dualcasting: Bravo's Gay Programming and the Quest for Women Audiences." *Cable Visions: Television Beyond Broadcasting*, Sarah Banet-Weiser, Cynthia Chris and Anthony Freitas, eds. (New York: New York University Press, 2007), 302–18.

Smith, Erin Copple. "'Affluencers' by Bravo: Defining an Audience Through Cross-Promotion." *Popular Communication* 10 (2012):4, 286–301.

Tasker, Yvonne and Diane Negra, eds. *Interrogating Postfeminism: Gender and the Politics of Popular Culture* (Durham, NC: Duke University Press, 2007), 1–26.

Traister, Rebecca. "The Single American Woman." *New York Magazine* February 22, 2016.

Warner, Kristen J. "'They Gon' Think You Loud Regardless: Ratchetness, Reality Television, and Black Womanhood." *Camera Obscura* 88, 30.1 (2015): 129–53.

Warner, Kristen J. "'Who Gon Check Me Boo': Reality TV as Haven for Black Women's Affect." *Flow TV* 14.6 (2011).

Weber, Brenda, ed. "*Reality Gendervisions: Sexuality and Gender on Transatlantic Reality TV* (Durham, NC: Duke University Press, 2014).

Weidhase, Nathalie. "'Beyoncé Feminism' and the Contestaion of the Black Feminist Body." *Celebrity Studies* 6.1 (Online January 2015): 128–31.

Wilson, Julie and Emily Chivers Yoachim. "Mothering Through Precarity: Becoming Mamapreneurial." *Cultural Studies* 29.5–6 (2015): 669–86.

Zuk, Tanya D. "'Proud Mormon Polygamist': Assimilation, Popular Memory, and the Mormon Churches in *Big Love*." *Journal of Religion and Popular Culture* 26.1 (Spring 2014): 93–106.

Index

Printed in the United States
By Bookmasters